Nordisk *Nordic*
Mad *Food*

TIME AND PLACE IN NORDIC CUISINE

René Redzepi

Photographs by
Ditte Isager

CONTENTS

MILK
SKIN
WITH
GRASS

Olafur Eliasson

Food is everything, but everything isn't always food

A plateful of milk skin with grass, flowers and herbs. That was one of the dishes on the day's menu. The garnish came from the field, where the cow that had supplied the milk had walked, grazed and defecated. The plate itself was a small closed ecosystem, which I ate my way through in some surprise (after all, it was a rather slimy-looking milk pancake with some greenery on top). There was no doubt about it: my mouth was exploring every area of the field.

Together with a group of friends and acquaintances, I consumed this dish one day in June 2007 during *Life in Space (LIS)* – an annual experimental workshop at my studio in Berlin. Here artists, architects, designers, social and natural scientists, and others meet to explore our experience of colour and movement, time and space. We make no distinction between experiments, discussions, drinking coffee and eating, and this informal framework usually results in a long succession of ideas, exercises, and an exploration of our senses. To prevent the meal appearing as a break from the themes of the day, I asked my friend René Redzepi if he might think about doing a number of experiments with food, which would have a bearing on our perception of time and space and which the *LIS* participants were to consume as we went along.

The milk skin recipe in particular aroused comment. Most people saw it as an extension of the day's topics; the milk skin was, as it were, stretched out into the other experiments. A central theme of *Life in Space* is how we experience space as a process – and not least about how we represent space in motion. To be able to do this, we need to integrate the idea, the work, the space, ourselves and the world around us into a single system. Aesthetic, social and political values come to influence one another – and the organic milk skin with 'all the good things of the field' was undoubtedly an extension of this line of thought. We do not stop the world when we eat; we go into it a little more deeply.

Since then I have had the opportunity to work closely with René again. We have discussed what cooking means when the building blocks are not pre-defined but emerge through experimentation with raw ingredients, consistency, colour, temperature and texture. The alphabet of food is not supplied in advance, but crafted as part of the actual work, and the relationships between the individual letters are created during the experimental journey.

Our conversations concerned memories of tastes and how taste is closely connected to images of places, moods, times and people.

When you work with a language of very delicate shades of meaning – in cooking as well as in art – it gives access to a subtle and unfamiliar register of experience. You come close to the limits of your sensory values. The senses combine, stretching your brain, and a new synaesthetic map appears.

We are constantly confronted with a trivialized sensory world, largely the product of banal commercialization. The makers of that world aim for 'safe' sensations, selling experiences with which their target group can immediately identify. As a result, the individual's imaginative ability is levelled off to become the same for everyone. The senses are blunted. By contrast, what is continually being developed at Noma helps to keep our senses keen. Its ability to surprise and sow the seeds of uncertainty is of the essence. You might say that Noma offers its guests a new language, but this language only acquires meaning by virtue of our personal way of using it – that is, through our individual experiences of taste (this also applies to good art: it simultaneously creates meaning and investigates the meaning it creates).

Take René's milk and field experiment during *Life in Space*. Without any great fuss, everyone was served the same dish. We were all in the same room, but we had vastly different experiences of what we were consuming. Something unique is happening here. A person has only one set of taste buds – they may react to sweet rather than savoury – and they may associate certain images or moods with the dish they are eating. Their expectations and scale of perception are specific to them. Their body ingests and converts the food in one particular way, whereas I have a different set of taste buds, a different body, a different previous history, and therefore a different experience. The difference we experience helps to emphasize that it is all about experimentation at a high level. It concerns an event that prioritizes individual perception within a space that is very much collective – the meal, the act of eating together.

We have grown up as part of a tradition that sees the eating of food as an isolated phenomenon, as an interval or a pause during the day. The food may be beautifully served; a miniature work of art that is detached from its surroundings by its pedestal – the plate. But this offers an impoverished taste experience.

Think of a tree. Some people will see it as an object in the landscape; its leaves have a particular shape, its bark a particular thickness. This kind of description may make it easier for a nursery to sell it. But of course the tree is not a detached object but part of a gigantic ecosystem: it is bound up with the soil in which it is growing, the rain and the sun. The process of photosynthesis makes it an essential component of our environment. The tree is part of the earth's lungs and is therefore inseparable from its surroundings. It has temporality built into it. A before and after. A summer, autumn, winter and spring.

In the same way, the potato cannot be separated from the soil in which it has grown. René knows that. That is why, later that day, the *LIS* participants also sank their teeth into another of his creations, the 'Newly-Ploughed Potato Field'–a dish of brownish– black, knobbly, crunchy food. And, just like the tree and the potato, the meal on the plate is part of a bigger system: the ingredients often belong to a particular season, they have a specific ripening process–their own temporal dimension–and they take a certain time to make their way through our bodies. They come from a field, a tree, a bush, an animal, the sea... In other words, they, like us, are inseparable from the environment. And Noma's environment is largely Scandinavian.

Food is just so commonplace. Everyone eats, everyone has an opinion about food. But taste is not exclusively a matter of individual perception, and food is never 'just food'. Whether we like it or not, what we eat affects how the world looks. And that affects the way we understand it. When we look at a plate of food, we should see the greater ecosystem too. If we find out where the food comes from and where it goes to, maybe this knowledge can be made into a kind of flavour-enhancer. It matters whether the potatoes come from New Zealand or from the Lammefjord area of Denmark, and I can see great potential in not dividing knowledge and flavour (just as in art, we should not separate form and content). They can be part of one and the same food experience. In the same way, cooking and eating and taste are associated with many other things. Food can be political. Food can be about responsibility, sustainability, geography and culture.

It is in the implementation of René's ideas that we find the integration of the experience of dining and the social dimension, of memories, cultural spaces, the raw ingredients of the Nordic countries, individual and collective experiences. I hope you will experience some of the same things when you make use of this book.

THE
PERFECT
STORM

Rune Skyum-Nielsen

The Story of Noma

In August 2003, three Danes set out on a literally and metaphorically breathtaking study tour of the North Atlantic. The trio consisted of the chefs René Redzepi and Mads Refslund plus the cookery writer, television personality and entrepreneur Claus Meyer. They were on an unusual seventeen-day mission to the Faroe Islands, Greenland and Iceland. The purpose was to absorb gastronomic inspiration and meet possible suppliers of raw materials and décor for what was, as far as we know, the first restaurant with a modern, North Atlantic menu.

René Redzepi, who was then just twenty-five years old, had been appointed chef of a Copenhagen restaurant that didn't yet have a name. To keep tabs on the new sensations with which the team expected to be bombarded, he had decided before setting out that, for the first time in his life, he would keep a diary.

When you read his detailed and often poetic reflections on the innumerable visits to smokehouses, potteries, illicit distilleries, fishing boats, fish factories and fish restaurants, you are immediately struck by his inspiration and drive. With just three months to go until the opening, René was hungrier than he had ever been. You can sense the euphoria in the lines he wrote on day eleven of the expedition, when the Danes were about to leave Iceland and head for Greenland. 'Everywhere we seemed to meet creative people, who were always busy planning ahead. I want to take this energy home with me to Denmark – along with the skyr, the cod, the halibut and the smelt roe, of course. Thank you, Iceland' wrote René on his laptop as the plane headed off towards its next North Atlantic destination.

Seven months later, something had happened to René's self-confidence and appetite. It was now March 2004 and he was once again walking over the inland ice of Greenland, where the biting temperature of minus 55°C penetrated his chest so that it hurt to breathe. Actually, he had been hurting for some time – ever since Noma, as the restaurant came to be called (a contraction of the Danish words *nordisk* and *mad*, meaning 'Nordic food'), had opened on a quayside at the outer edge of Christianshavn, the most beautiful and unspoilt quarter of old Copenhagen.

It was Claus Meyer who had offered René the opportunity to become chef and a partner, along with himself and the entrepreneur Kristian Byrge, in this new venture. It was to be located in a warehouse dating from 1767 known as Nordatlantens Brygge (the North Atlantic Wharf) – the cultural centre for Iceland, Greenland and the Faroes in the Danish capital. When Claus was given the opportunity to create a restaurant in its rough, lofty rooms, there was one requirement. The restaurant was to reflect Nordic, especially North Atlantic, cuisine. There was no alternative, given its location and the history of the building.

At that time, René had first refusal on a number of other tempting offers. It was rare for such a young man to be offered the position of chef in several of the country's top restaurants, yet he chose to accept the biggest and riskiest of the challenges. However, it was a hesitant acceptance, because there was a mental barrier to cross. When René thought of North Atlantic cuisine, his ideas were automatically restricted. For example, what would he do during the long harsh winter if everything had to be grown outdoors? And what on earth would he use as substitutes for the traditional herbs? 'I soon realized that I had to cast an eye over other regional cuisines to find inspiration for how to run a North Atlantic restaurant. There wasn't really any experience to draw on in Denmark or the rest of Scandinavia, where the restaurants don't base their philosophy on their own regions and their own cultural heritage. The problem was simply that French and Spanish restaurants had a completely different set of raw materials to work with. So it was a big mental challenge, which made me have doubts about the project and consider other job opportunities,' Rene admits.

The rest of the Danish restaurant world laughed at Noma's gastronomic concept. Even some of René's closest allies in the profession poured scorn on these insubstantial visions and gave the restaurant nicknames like 'Blubber Restaurant', the 'Whale Penis' and the 'Seal-Fucker'. Messing about with traditional Nordic food and raw materials was not the done thing. It was ridiculous. 'People dismissed us as a mere flash in the pan,' René explains. 'By contrast, my view was that we had the chance to create our own way of expressing ourselves, our own signature. The fact that I wasn't taking over an existing business and wouldn't have to carry on and work in the spirit of an old restaurant tipped the scales.'

When you stick your head above the parapet you do risk being shot at, particularly in Denmark, where there is a long-standing adherence to what the writer Aksel Sandemose called *Janteloven* – the Scandinavian equivalent of the tall poppy syndrome. René and Claus's Nordic restaurant project was quite daring. It could justifiably be said that Noma's prospects of success lay in the fact that respect for Danish cuisine was at rock bottom, both at home and abroad. Those willing to take risks had everything to gain, because the Danes had more or less given up. They were not making the most of their raw materials, and pasta had overtaken potatoes as the most popular ingredient of the evening meal. Danish food was not talked about with pride and when cooking at home or eating out Danes looked mainly towards southern Europe.

'Well on into the 1990s, Danish food was still associated with insipid gravy, boiled potatoes and grey burgers. At that time, good chefs in Denmark didn't have a polite word to say about Danish food either. It had to be either French or Italian', says the food historian Bi Skaarup. In her view, the post-war boom in the export of meat and dairy produce to Britain helped to undermine Danish food culture. All the nice things were rushed over the English Channel, so that the Danes were left with second-class goods as Bi puts it: 'They were no longer self-sufficient down on the farms either. They sent the top-quality butter abroad, while they made do with margarine from the local, not very inviting, supermarket – because, if you ate your own butter, you would lose the income from selling it.'

Danish food, indeed Nordic food in general, was non-existent in terms of international gastronomy, and with good reason. When the food connoisseur Bent Christensen contacted the Michelin Guide in the early 1970s and suggested charting the Danish restaurant scene, he was told that there was probably not a single restaurant worth visiting. However, Bent didn't think the situation was that bad and wrote his own *Danish Food Guide*, which has been issued annually ever since.

He notes that the experience of eating out in restaurants was given a real boost in the 1980s by the celebrity chefs Søren Gericke and Erwin Lauterbach. Although both had trained in France, they liked to talk loud and long about making good use of Danish raw materials and scrapping the obligatory foie gras. The opportunity to haul Danish gastronomy out of the backwaters must not be missed, they urged. Today's go-getting Danish Michelin-starred chefs acknowledge the inspiration they derived from the grand old men of new Danish cuisine, but at that time their impact on the public was limited.

'They were so far ahead of the field they almost lost contact with Danish food culture and the Danish public. We are readier to learn from the top chefs now', says Bi Skaarup. René Redzepi remembers Søren Gericke's television appearances very well. This pioneer didn't make a great impression on him at the time, nor did he inspire him until many years later. When René was a schoolboy, cookery was just another compulsory subject on the timetable, like mathematics. And he wasn't the only one who felt like that. Preparing fancy food just wasn't something that appealed to the Danes at that time. When René ate at his schoolmates' homes, they had ready-made food such as oven chips or a Chinese takeaway.

'It was fast rather than decent,' René recalls, though he had learnt a little more about food from his Macedonian father, whose attitude to raw materials and their preparation was different from that of most Danish people – he knew all the basics. 'A lot has changed since then. My gut feeling tells me that the speed of information partly explains the increasing interest the Danes have shown in gourmet cuisine. When I went to restaurant school as a fifteen-year-old [in 1993] we were still an ignorant nation when it came to gastronomy. Now it has become a kind of status symbol to be interested in cooking. It is no longer just a matter for professionals, and in certain circles it is considered almost uneducated not to know anything about food. It's a bit like jazz, isn't it? You really ought to know a little bit about it.'

Bent Christensen can plainly see signs that the Danes are now being directly inspired by their home-grown elite chefs. 'But it's one small step at a time, and there's still a long way to go', says this author of many books on top Danish and international restaurants. 'Wild garlic is used in ordinary households now, and it has gradually become acceptable to use root vegetables in cooking. On the suppliers' side, there is a growing interest in the old, forgotten regional Danish cheeses, and local cider factories are also springing up. Some of these trends can be explained as a definite Noma effect. We are becoming more and more interested in what we can do ourselves.'

However, back in 2003 it was still an uphill struggle to convince anybody that a restaurant serving Scandinavian food had any legitimacy at all. René Redzepi was particularly irritated by the teasing of his fellow professionals, but, working almost twenty-four hours a day during the six months before opening, he chose to use their scepticism as fuel when the hill was steepest.

On the way, he had managed to find the architect Signe Bindslev, who was commissioned to furnish the rooms, find furniture of classic Danish design and design new pieces to match. Everything was made of natural materials: iron, stone, wood and clay. No seven-branched candelabra, but Scandinavian simplicity that wouldn't put the food in the shade. Rather than expensive silverware and porcelain, the round tables were laid with different kinds of plates and knives, and even daggers. 'After all, nothing is exactly the same,' says René, 'unless it comes off a factory conveyor belt. Many restaurants also have logos everywhere, on napkins, plates and glasses, as if the guests don't know where they are. Nothing of that sort ever came up. It's a kind of "McDonaldization", which is not in the spirit of Noma. We would rather signal that our priority is the food and how it is served.'

Despite the thorough preparations, after a mere three months things weren't going well for René Redzepi and Noma. The reviews were good but by no means effusive, and Noma didn't stand out as strikingly different. The restaurant wasn't perceived as a stylish new creation, but rather as a utopian intermezzo, and although his CV was formidable by Danish standards, René Redzepi had proved to be only human. It was a place to eat that people had to visit once at most, just so they could say they had been there.

The mental barrier that had affected René in the start-up phase was now flourishing among his potential customers: 'People were busy asking me why I wanted to restrict my culinary options. After all, we were in a gastronomic age in which anything was possible, and everything was just beginning. If you wanted to make a dish with oranges in it, you put in oranges, and that was it. The criticism we received made me clearly understand that whole unrestricted way of thinking.'

Personally, René felt anything but human. He is such a perfectionist that the lukewarm reception made him feel wretched, and when he got home he would flop down on the sofa and fall asleep with exhaustion – if his troubles would allow him to sleep at all. He wasn't eating properly and had quarrelled with Mads Refslund – his sous-chef and closest friend – who had elected to leave Noma after the first two hectic months. 'My frustration increased. I didn't think we were doing anything in a different way, and I couldn't see myself spending the rest of my life as a chef. It was altogether too unsatisfactory', says René of his most profound professional and personal crisis. So now he was back in Greenland, on his first so-called holiday for years. The workaholic René Redzepi had decided to go to the inland ice to shoot musk oxen with the hunters who supplied Noma with game.

At the expedition's camp near Sønderstrøm Fjord nothing happened aside from the alternation between long nights and short days, and René had all the time in the world to ponder on what was wrong with his restaurant. The rugged surroundings did him good. While an icy snowstorm raged outside the hut, the awareness of Greenland's magnificent, almost uninhabited landscape crept up on him. He thought of the rest of the vast Scandinavian landmass with its population of a mere 25 million. Noma's guests should experience the unique unspoilt nature of the North. They should become aware of time and place and follow the conditions that govern existence in these regions, with sharp changes in the range of available raw materials from spring to summer, summer to autumn, autumn to winter and winter to spring; from being flooded with light to stumbling about in the dark, from airy abundance to bone-numbing cold.

'I realized that we had to exploit the seasons in a better way, so that you could only get a particular dish here and now. We should explore the extremes of nature, seek out the thousand or more species of edible fungi, the many wild plants, roots and seashore plants. That became the embryo of an idea. The guests dining at Noma should feel a sensation of time and place in their very bones. That was to be the starting point, the core, the first layer. There would follow a number of extra layers of conceptual thoughts about the dishes, such as innovation, technique and the right staff', explains René. In his diary he noted down ideas and created the first dishes, starting with a particular ingredient and combining it with items from its natural habitat. If venison was on the menu, the meat should be served with snails, pine shoots and mushrooms. 'It all began to make sense. A connection appeared between our place, the way the food is arranged on the plates, and how it is served. It no longer felt pretentious; it felt right.'

According to René himself, Noma's breakthrough came about when he finally jettisoned his baggage from the years at elBulli in Roses, Catalonia, the French Laundry in San Francisco, Le Jardin des Sens in Montpellier and the Kong Hans in Copenhagen, the last-named for many years the leader among Danish restaurants with its French-inspired cuisine. 'I realized that I had gone about things the wrong way during Noma's first months. A gastronomic supermeal didn't necessarily have to involve the things I had brought with me from the top kitchens in other parts of the world. I recognized that I didn't have the necessary mental freedom, and that was what I had to find', he says. In addition, in its first few months Noma had been hampered by its location in the Nordatlantens Brygge in Christianshavn. The geographical connection had been taken too literally, and this reduced the kitchen's room to manoeuvre. The concept became too narrow, too confined, and that was how the food tasted. For example, Greenland halibut had been on the menu right from the start, even if it meant that it had to be transported frozen to Copenhagen. 'That would never happen today,' says René. 'Instead of taking home a frozen fish, we would scan our own Danish waters and invest in a freshly caught turbot from one of the fishing boats at Gilleleje, less than 30 kilometres north of Copenhagen. After all, the whole point is to give the guests the best possible impression of the season here and now, so why should we import fish from Greenland that might just as well have been caught eight months ago? Freezing can also mean that the fish loses flavour and texture.'

However, it was the time he had spent at elBulli, Le Jardin des Sens and Kong Hans in particular that blocked René's attempts to make his mark on Noma's menu during the first few months. He automatically composed the dishes as he had seen them done at these restaurants. Although the dishes were always given a Scandinavian twist as far as the ingredients were concerned, he was basically not making Scandinavian food.

'The tragic-comedic thing about it was that I actually left elBulli with a feeling of freedom. Having the freedom to do what I wanted. But when I opened a restaurant myself, I just used a few of the basic ideas from there instead of making good use of my freedom. We hadn't found our own signature, not even taken a preliminary run at it. I wasn't listening enough to myself. Instead I went over to established routines – things that were already in existence and meaningful. Routines that I knew from experience would work, because they had done so at the places where I had previously been. At Le Jardin des Sens, the majority of dishes used a stock-based sauce, so to start with I created a Scandinavian cuisine that had a strong flavour of liquids that had been reduced and simmered. This is all right in individual dishes, but pouring reduced chicken stock over boiled Jerusalem artichokes seems pointless to me now. After all, it doesn't taste much of artichoke then, and instead of a link to the natural habitat of the raw material, the dish acquires a meaty element. The same was true of many of our soups. If we were going to make a pumpkin soup, we automatically added chicken stock. We don't any more', says René emphatically.

He also used many variations on elBulli's fondness for decon-structing classic dishes – only now with a strong Scandinavian character. The way the pioneering Catalan restaurant would typically dream up what looked like a familiar carbonara, but in which the fettucini deceived the eye and were really made of a jellified mild chicken stock, was used by the Noma chefs to redefine a classic Danish dish of garnished cod. The raw materials were still largely the same, but the melted butter might be replaced by a beetroot sauce. Traditionally beetroot would have been served pickled as part of a heavy garnish, but in the early days of Noma the other vegetables were arranged on top of the fish in a way that created the illusion of a living environment.

'We made a lot of that kind of thing. We also served *biksemad* [a legendary Danish dish, a kind of fry-up made with meat and potatoes left over from the previous day's dinner]. But of course it was made from scratch and with Norway lobsters. To begin with, it felt very meaningful to do things that way', says René.

A typical example of how he gave his culinary baggage a Scandinavian accent would be dispensing with caramelizing a crème brûlée and also adding a spot of sea buckthorn to the dessert. It might taste wonderful, but it was definitely not original nor true to its geographical latitudes. 'The dish had too strong a link to something with a completely different history and background', he admits six years later.

While the snowstorm continued to rage over the Greenland ice in March 2004, René continued to brainstorm. Page after page it came together, with ideas for new dishes, jottings about what was missing from the old ones, and a number of attempts to define the essence of Noma. Fundamentally, it concerned his first two ideas: it was about time and place and about reconstructing habitats.

'We pared it to the bone and made everything more transparent – more straightforward. If we had one special ingredient, we surrounded it with the foodstuffs it lived among or on, for instance wild boar with corn and berries. It brought real meaning into my world, and at that moment I knew for certain that we would get the upper hand. It was no longer just food on a plate. There was a story contained in it. And that train of thought reminded me in many ways of my childhood summers in Macedonia, where we lived mainly on local vegetables. My family never had much money, so down there we ate what we grew ourselves.'

Straightforwardness is also evident in the very unpretentious names the Noma chefs give their dishes. A glance at the restaurant's constantly changing menu is a study in straight talking. Take for example a dish that consists mainly of milk and dill. It is, of course, called 'Milk and Dill'. 'The things we do should preferably speak for themselves', explains René. 'The greatest form of gastronomic beauty occurs when the guests themselves have the experience, instead of us taking them by the hand and giving them idealized input. They must create their own image of the experience, so it becomes more than just a nice taste.'

René has since dubbed his diary of the North Atlantic study tour in August 2004 'The Perfect Storm'. 'This is an expression that fishermen use about the kind of storms when sky and sea melt into one, but everything works well all the same. The fishermen know they will come through it all right. And that's how Noma feels, as we manoeuvre through the hectic waters of challenges and the pressure of expectations. In our case, the waves and gusts have simply been replaced by ingredients, dishwashers, trainee waiters and so on. You could say that our study tour was the starting signal for a storm that is still raging. A storm I love being in the middle of.'

About a year after René's brainwave among the Greenland ice, Noma received its first Michelin star. It was a cherished reward for the kitchen team to have its pioneering work recognized by such an illustrious institution. By that time Redzepi and Company had long been receiving signals from the outside world that the restaurant was on the way out of its backwater as part of a new theme in international gastronomic circles – a theme that would soon become known as 'the Nordic way'. The intervals between expressions of criticism and disappointment from the guests became longer and longer, and praise increased in inverse proportion. These reactions were a huge relief for someone like René Redzepi, who needs a hundred pats on the back to eclipse a single shake of the head.

'There was a striking difference in people's enthusiasm,' he says.

'When they were served steak tartare, the effect was quite different from when we used to serve Jerusalem artichoke soup on chicken stock with scallops. I suddenly had the feeling that most Scandinavians recognized something in our food – something from their childhood. Everyone has tried walking round a lake, where the dead leaves crunch under your feet – or at any rate they have visited a farm. A visit to Noma should reflect these experiences, and many Scandinavians have told me that a meal in our restaurant reminded them of something lying hidden way back in their memory. Maybe they tasted the same gooseberries while walking in the woods as a child. For foreigners it also suddenly made sense to visit a restaurant with a Scandinavian-based cuisine. They had an experience they couldn't get at home. Several have said that it was like hearing a new language and being able to understand what was being said.'

This experience has also gradually taken root among colleagues and others in the profession, most recently exemplified by Noma's number one position in *Restaurant* magazine's prestigious ranking list, the S. Pellegrino World's Fifty Best Restaurants. This top rank does not surprise Frenchman Andrea Petrini, an internationally recognized writer on cultural matters and one of the judges of the awards. 'Noma was in the right place at the right time, but 90 per cent of the so-called gastronomic elite have gone on to autopilot and are simply repeating themselves,' says Petrini. He visited Noma for the first time in summer 2004 and the number of his return visits now runs into double figures. His first impression was that everything was perfect, and he refuses to pick out any individual dish or experience at Noma. 'That would be a very over-simplified approach,' he says. 'Everything should be highlighted: the concept, the solidarity, the philosophy. "The comfort of strangeness", as the author Ian McEwan might say. It completely changed my image of what a restaurant can be capable of. As Pierre Gaignaire's restaurant did in 1985, and Ferran Adrià did with elBulli in 1991.' In his opinion René Redzepi is unique, and he sums up his craft in these words, 'It is sharp and fresh and takes things back to the roots and the soil. His culinary art is characterized by an utter crystalline limpidity and "readability".'

Like so many others, before his first visit to Noma Andrea Petrini knew nothing about Scandinavian cuisine except for the Swedish chef Mathias Dahlgren. Now he believes in a future for Noma and the succession of related restaurants that have arrived on the scene in recent years. It is a future that the creators of elBulli also predicted a few years ago, 'Hopefully, Noma will be a never-ending story, and I feel certain that we will be able to skim through the first chapter right now. Ferran Adrià has said half-jokingly that the future of the modern culinary art will come from the Nordic countries. He has been proved to be right.'

When Saturday turns into Sunday and all but the the last few guests have left the restaurant after twelve to sixteen courses, Noma's chefs gather at the front of the five-section kitchen. Despite the fact that they have just finished a working day of twelve hours or more, the concentration deepens. The twenty-five or so people involved would not miss this ritual for anything, and with good reason. It gives them a chance to try out their own creations in front of a team of chefs that is currently one of the most hyped and celebrated in the world, and the opportunity to gain a better understanding of how a dish is created in René Redzepi's head.

The Noma staff dedicate the next few hours to a joint brainstorming and tasting session, at which everyone from apprentices to the second-in-command can have some input and express an honest opinion. They take it in turns: one chef from each section presents a dish each Saturday night. So everyone gets a chance sooner or later, and usually not more than four or five weeks go by before their turn to produce the food comes around again.

This session has also become an attraction for the restaurant's regular, most dedicated guests. They gather together, murmuring, in front of the glass partition, watching the group of cooks who are concentrating so hard that they have forgotten to look tired after yet another strenuous week.

This Saturday session has been a permanent, and indeed compulsory, feature of the cooks' training since autumn 2005. René sees the gathering as one of most important fixed points in a hectic working life, where the pressure just goes on increasing as Noma gets better. 'It is crucial that our staff develop during their time here and don't only contribute their labour and professional skill,' he says. 'If good people come to Copenhagen to be a part of our project, they must get something in return.'

The first of the evening's six presentations on this Saturday in March 2010 is the responsibility of Blaine, an American chef from the cold section. He has frozen inside a block of ice one of the nets in which Noma's fresh mussels are usually delivered. The raw mussels are arranged on top and surrounded by seaweed and pickled cabbage. There is enough for everybody to be able to taste this creation.

Immediately people begin to comment. René knows from experience that he should hold back so that his opinion doesn't influence the others and people get to train their palates and their ability to put into words what they have actually sensed. 'We train our people to get better at tasting. This will benefit them, and it's a bonus for our guests that the chefs are able to express what they experience and generally respond to the food. I have been surprised to find that many of the chefs, who come to our kitchen from some of the best restaurants in the world, don't really know what they actually like about food. They are all trained to perform and deliver, not to think independently about a particular dish or raw material. They follow the recipe instead of just using it as a firm reference point. It's a problem, because when it comes down to it, it is the experienced chefs – themselves – who add the magic', says René.

He emphasizes the fact that the Saturday sessions are not there to drain the chefs of their knowledge; on the contrary, the dishes they present very rarely end up on the menu. They are exclusively for the purpose of fostering the kitchen staff's ability to form independent attitudes to food and to make their responses a little less automatic. 'Better cooks produce better food – it really is as simple as that',

maintains the head chef, who takes it seriously if a cook doesn't get involved in the collective development, 'That annoys me intensely. People must seize their chance to improve. Noma must not stand still, and we don't do that as individuals in the kitchen either. If you come and present a new dish with the words, "I really don't like it myself", I say that I have a family at home and I'd love to be able to get up an hour or two later on Sunday morning to be with my wife and child.'

All the same, it's unusual for the cooks not to make the effort, and back in the open kitchen Blaine's colleagues like the mussel arrangement. The American receives high-fives and cries of delight. The criticism, even the few negative comments, is constructive. René too expresses distinct satisfaction. He praises the dish for its poetic overall impression and its flavour, and because it has a strong link to the persistent icy winter that still reigns outside. After all, cabbage and mussels are among the few raw materials available to play with before the arrival of spring. However, the head chef also comments that the dish looks a bit 'like scraps'. He would like to have had even more seaweed and twigs in the composition.

Then it's the turn of the next cook, who has had homework to do, and five presentations later it's finally time to go home. It's nearly three o'clock, and the team open a few beers before going off into the night. René and his sous-chefs remain to assess the past week before he strides over to his bicycle and pedals home to his sleeping family on the other side of the bridge between Christianshavn and the inner city.

Noma's chefs don't only have to be able to present a dish to their colleagues. Every evening they are detailed to serve the guests in the restaurant. All the chefs, without exception. The waiters are responsible for the majority of the service, but when a dish is presented at table it is often one of the people who created it that brings it in. This is René's own idea and it was introduced early on in Noma's existence. Personally, he had never particularly cared for the ritual of having to go out and shake hands with the guests when the meal was over. It seemed too artificial, too stiff and formal. 'But I wanted to go out into the restaurant and say hello, so instead I presented one or two dishes at each table – without introducing myself. Then if any of the guests were especially pleased and asked to speak to the chef, they were a bit surprised to recognize me as one of their waiters. It created a different mood for them as they went home and also aroused something in me. After all, by serving the food myself I get an impression of whether everything is as it should be at the tables', René explains.

This unpretentious way of serving food has become one of Noma's special features, and René believes that it might very well start a new trend. 'I don't care about great armies of waiters in dinner jackets and bow ties manoeuvring their way through luxurious surroundings. When I go out to eat, I want to spot the qualities that make the place unique. And one of Noma's qualities is that we are down to earth. Even though many people see us as a restaurant that is storming ahead, we are also casual in the sense that everybody is welcome here and we don't have cloths on the tables. You don't get a posh atmosphere at Noma.

We hope you get a pure and unpretentious experience, and the staff help to create this mood by meeting the guests on an equal footing. By having the cooks serve the food we demonstrate that, when it comes down to it, it's all about their handiwork and not the packaging. Maybe we risk a few slight imperfections now and then, which would not happen with our trained waiters, but I'm inclined to believe that this is setting a trend rather than holding us back, as this way our guests usually have a more exciting experience.'

René also thinks that the daily contact with the guests, like the late Saturday sessions, helps the cooks to hone their skills. 'When they can look the guests in the eye, it results in a much more concentrated effort than if they stand there peeling potatoes in a stainless steel-clad cellar. The long days, the extreme stress and the constant high level of concentration make it more meaningful for the cooks, who get to know one of the most humble and important elements of running a restaurant, namely the sensation and emotion of giving. And at the same time they realize that their work is appreciated', explains René.

Every month, sometimes every week or every day, Noma is subject to the vagaries of the season, so changes to the menu are gradual but constant. The tempo is dictated by the availability of raw materials. As a result, there is no fixed structure to the compilation of a menu. All the same, René endeavours to keep some degree of consistency. 'I like to see a high degree of energy about the tempo at which the guests encounter the dishes. A lot has to happen at the start, so people notice that they have come to a dynamic eating place. We take care of this by putting out a whole lot of small mood creators in the form of appetizers, until the guests have decided whether to go for a menu of anywhere from four to sixteen courses.'

During the protein-rich Scandinavian winter this isn't always easy to do, but at other times Noma's chefs like to start the menus with a seafood repertoire. Next come the courses that are easier to prepare and the partly pre-cooked courses, where vegetables play an important part. Then the desserts usher in the finale.

'You would not be served an overly filling and heavily cooked series of courses in Noma,' says René. 'A piece of braised meat is of course fully prepared, but everything around it leads towards an overall impression of something light and succulent. When you leave Noma, you must of course go away satisfied, but there is a big difference between feeling you have eaten too much and feeling pleasantly full and in a light state of mind. The menu is constructed in such a way that you arrive at that state step-by-step. We create the refreshing sensation of lots of juice and tartness in the mouth by using many more vegetables, berries, herbs and wild plants than you see in most other restaurants. And that's how I prefer it myself. If I have plenty of time, that's the kind of menu I put together at home for my wife, our daughter and myself.'

The courses are arranged so that the ingredients are in keeping with their original habitat – raw and unpretentious. As René says, it's not very meaningful to cut root vegetables into harlequin patterns just to show that the cooks can achieve millimetre accuracy. 'I simply

can't see the link to the natural environment of the raw material if it's served up looking like a chessboard. We serve the food organically, so it tastes of where it comes from and looks like what it is, as if there's a connecting thread running from the natural product through to the way it's prepared. It also shows that we respect our raw materials.'

Although René still faces a number of challenges, not least on the supplier side, he feels happier about Noma's future prospects than ever before. The routines and thought processes of his previous workplaces no longer haunt Noma's menu, and that is absolutely crucial: 'We have long since found our own way, and we know which taste experiences we want to leave the guests with. Now it's all up to us. Our challenge for many years to come will lie more in continuing to innovate and in maintaining our inspiration, so we don't go round in circles and repeat ourselves. The autopilot is our worst enemy. For the first three or four years we developed month by month, week by week – sometimes day by day. New dishes were created in a single evening. It no longer happens at such breathless speed, even though we still take great satisfaction in seeking out and reconnoitering new territory. For the guests, visiting Noma has simply got better. The experience is more coherent and rounded. When we come across new raw materials today, it's easier to decode them. However, it's still a challenge – fortunately.'

The Raw Materials through the Seasons

It's no use dwelling on the seasons when you are expounding on the subject of Scandinavian raw materials. Not nostalgically, at any rate. Every season has its charms, its characteristics, and that's part of what makes life in Noma's kitchen a dynamic affair. 'I am very fond of winter, but in the end I find I get tired of it,' admits René. 'Then spring comes as a relief, but some time in May I also start to look forward to the summer and the taste of strawberries. And then suddenly you find yourself missing the taste of nuts and mushrooms.' Raw materials are deceitful flirts who abandon you, die on you and make room for new acquaintances. They are, to a great extent, the justification for Noma's existence – both its Achilles heel and a blessing.

René has come to terms with the harsh, weather-beaten realities. In fact he wouldn't have it any other way. The constant changes mean that the restaurant never stands still and prevent him and his colleagues in the kitchen from lulling themselves to sleep. 'In many ways it's a cliché when chefs say that without raw materials you have nothing. But it's certainly true for us. The raw materials are king, and that's why we are so dependent on the people who grow, collect and transport them. We must have the absolute best raw materials that, even in the simple ways we serve them, can do something that other raw materials cannot do', he explains.

During Noma's first six years, the restaurant has built up a supplier network of sixty or seventy collectors, fishermen, dry goods stores, dairymen and farmers, who continually call in to say what they have to offer or can get hold of on their way. 'They are all extremely enthusiastic, and without them we wouldn't be very different from all the other restaurants out there. So my great dream is to be able to employ a dedicated sous-chef just for the raw materials – someone who can ensure that we maintain the best possible relations with our suppliers. We are happy to make a special effort in order to be a special working partner for all these invaluable people', says René.

When spring sets in, Noma changes course completely. Typically, the first sign of the new season is the supplier of lumpfish roe reporting his first productive catches. This means that the sea temperature is rising, and René knows that the wild garlic will soon be shooting up out of the ground. 'Wild garlic is the ultimate harbinger of spring,' he explains. 'It tastes of lots of things. It's a product that grows wild and only arrives when Mother Earth says: "Now is the moment. Now it's time to kick-start the spring." For a chef, quite simply, it's one of the best days of the year.'

The staff themselves find many of the raw materials that make Noma's repertoire so exceptional. At dawn during the days in March the chef and a team of his cooks set off for the most untamed of the Copenhagen parks, a mere ten or fifteen minutes' cycle ride from the restaurant, where the wildlife is left to flourish as it likes. In temperatures of 8–10°C the team pick the first shoots of wild garlic, which taste mild and green with a hint of both garlic and chives – anything but winter. 'Biting into the first shoots is quite simply fantastic. If you are lucky, you will also find the first March violets in the same batch.'

A few weeks later, the Noma chefs bring different greenstuff home in their duffle bags: wild plants that have for many years been regarded as weeds, but nevertheless taste of something. The yellow star of Bethlehem peeps out now, and the chickweed is just beginning to get sweet enough. Other so-called weeds, such as garlic mustard, announce their arrival and the chefs keep on picking until their hands are aching with the cold and the thought of a cup of scalding hot tea in the Noma kitchen is just too tempting. 'These expeditions are not like anything I have experienced at other restaurants. There is something fantastic about living from season to season and being able to enjoy the changes in weather and temperature. Something fantastic about being pleased when it pours with rain for three days in succession. After all,' emphasises René Redzepi, 'it just means that the mushrooms are on their way!'

The next spring 'rebirth' is the arrival of vegetables. Farmers ring in, perhaps to say that the asparagus looks as though it has only two or three weeks to go and the pea shoots are on their way up. The fishermen also have news for Noma. Lots of shrimp have arrived in the fjords, rich in flavour yet surprisingly light. And turbot. And zander. And so on. A visit to the farms of Zealand reveals that the lambs have grown big enough, and that the milk tastes different because the cows are grazing in wide open spaces.

Then summer comes, and Noma turns its focus on the many wild plants that grow in Denmark and Sweden in particular. Summer is also the main season for preserving and pickling, and the Noma chefs help to collect 100 kilos of roses along the coasts. They also get 70 kilos of unripe elderberries and 60 kilos of wild garlic fruits. And then of course there are Danish strawberries – an essential national dish through the centuries, eaten just with cream.

Autumn is a strong candidate for René's own favourite season. At any rate it is the one that offers the most possibilities. The lush Scandinavian summer has abated, and now fungi are popping up all over the place on tree trunks and on the forest floor. With a bit of luck you can watch the head chef himself clambering about in the trees in the Dyrehaven park to the north of Copenhagen, where he can collect big clusters of oyster mushrooms growing 2–3 metres above the ground. Root vegetables are warming themselves in the rich soil, and bushes and trees are weighed down with berries and nuts. Lettuces are thriving, vegetables are bursting with juice and energy, and pumpkins are bulging. Autumn is truly a fruitful season in these latitudes. Winter is a much less predictable matter. When Scandinavia is hit by a very cold winter its native cuisine is up against it. 'We can find almost nothing,' René confirms. And yet, in the woods around Copenhagen and even in town gardens, wood sorrel, garden sorrel, chickweed and nettles are appearing all the same. 'You just have to know where to look', he adds. Noma's chefs – an increasingly international team as the restaurant's fame spreads around the world – queue up to join René in trips to farms, beaches and city parks to find ingredients for their dishes. 'It may sound like easy work, but all the cooks are immensely keen to go, whoever they are, and whatever country they come from. To go out into the countryside and pick your own ingredients is a rare phenomenon in international gastronomy, and that's a great shame.' According to René, this experience in the field changes the way the cooks act in the kitchen. When you get close to the raw materials and touch them while they are still one with nature, taste them at the moment they let go of the soil, you learn to respect them. As a result, there is never any question of altering the raw material to such an extent that, when it reaches its destination on the plate, it no longer has any connection with its origins.

'You have become aware of the history of the raw material or the farmer's passion and his involvement with the raw material he grows for you. This encounter means that you wouldn't dream of manipulating the materials excessively. It's about being able to feel the link to the producer, whether it's nature herself or agriculture. We only do our job properly if we succeed in creating a dish in which we show the history of the raw material and put it in the right context. Without this connection it makes no sense', René maintains.

RENÉ'S DIARY

A Norwegian fisherman once told me about the perfect storm. Most fishermen and sailors from his region have experienced it. It is a storm in which sky and sea seem to flow together, and Ragnarök (in Nordic mythology, the end of the world) is around the corner. Everything goes wrong. You are about to give up. But you continue, even though your strength is almost exhausted. The one thing that keeps you going is the feeling that everything will calm down. Your instinct tells you that everything will be OK, that there is control in spite of everything.

This makes a perfect analogy with my experience at Noma. Except that in my restaurant breakers and squalls are replaced by shifts, schedules, fat filters, computer viruses, emails, phone calls, floods, fire alarms, power cuts, bank employees, creditors, bad suppliers, bad debtors, current accounts, holiday pay, unions, labour market assessments, recipes, environmental health inspectors, the press, TV documentaries, newspaper front pages, jealousy, hiring staff, firing staff, stress, pressure...

The following pages are extracted from a diary that might be called 'The Start of the Storm'. They describe my first voyage of discovery in search of new produce . It was a trip to the North Atlantic – to the Faroes, Iceland and Greenland – in August 2003, three months before Noma's opening. I was twenty-five years old, very green, but as full of enthusiasm as I am today. I had never tried to keep a diary before, but I felt that, since I was to write about a great new chapter in my life, I could not document it as I normally did, with notes. Everything should be new.

Today I am very happy I did this. Unfortunately, I have not kept a diary since, and over the years I have in some odd way erased three days from it. Thus the story ends a little abruptly. But I hope that, even so, you will be able to share the enthusiasm and optimism I felt at that time.

This trip marked the start of Noma's kitchen. Here the contours of the future flavours were sketched out. If I had my doubts about the kitchen's sustainability at the outset, after the journey they were... mmmmmmm.

Mandag

We arrive at Tórshavn airport, in the Faroe Islands, at 10 a.m. local time. Incredible approach. Soft lush green cliffs everywhere. The air feels crisp and cleansing. Bus to the centre. We will be sleeping locally, at No. 28 Torsgøta, a small 1930s house. Pleasant little house. Very cosy. Actually nice not having to stay in a hotel.

First meeting is with Gunnar Hoydal, writer-poet who in 2003 was awarded the regional government's cultural prize. Quick low-down on the city of Tórshavn, and on Faroese history. Eat fish and chips for lunch. Have tasted better. I saw some very nice outdoor lamps which would be great to use in the warehouse. Made by architect Høgne Larsen.

Meet with Kjartan Kristiansen, the director of the Faroese Trade Council. We arrange to have dinner. Get picked up by Kjartan at 7 p.m. At his home, we meet his wife Inga. She has cooked the most incredible turnips ever. Just dug up from the garden. Sweet, soft and moist. Almost taste like pears. Why? Is it because of the cold climate with long days and correspondingly more sun in summer? A huge discovery!

I get acquainted with havtorn (Hippophae rhamnoides *or sea-buckthorn*). A small yellow-orange berry. Very, very sour. Tastes of exotic fruits. Wow! Would be good for syrup, sauces, aquavit, drying, savouries and desserts. Everything. We also taste revling (Empetrum nigrum *or crowberries*). They grow in a plantation in Hornbæk in Denmark, I am told. Not as interesting as sea-buckthorn. Classic Faroese style, as Inga had it as a child: tykmælk (soured milk) or cream, sugar and crowberries.

Kjartan introduces us to Gunnar 'Marnie' Simonsen. Great personality, fisherman to the bone. We drive to his little fishing cave, around 15 kilometres out of Tórshavn. Here we eat live langoustines. The shell is shaved from the tail, while trying to avoid the furious and desperate claws snapping at us. A little salt on the tail and in they go! You can still feel the meat pulsating in the mouth. The juice from the meat gels instantly on the lips. Wild! The tears are flowing. Claus is scared, but also sheds a tear. We taste them cooked too. They are very firm and sweet. Really tasty, without a doubt some of the nicest langoustines I have seen anywhere. They can weigh up to 400 grams each.

We also have a look at Gunnar's taskekrabber (Cancer pagurus *or edible crab*). Caught 1,200 metres deep (in Denmark you generally catch them 100–200 metres deep), meaning very cold water, which makes the meat extra-juicy, tasty, full of sweetness. Blindfolded, one could almost confuse this tasty meat for Danish lobster! A fantastic product. We absolutely must *have this seafood for the restaurant. We will try to get an aquarium/tank set up at Bryggen to keep them alive when we receive them.*

By 10p.m. we are back at the house. Spectacular first day. Kjartan and his wife. The sea-buckthorn berries, the turnips, the seafood. The meeting with Gunnar was the peak. I feel high on these great discoveries. Claus has kransekage (Danish almond cake) and Mads makes coffee. Goodnight.

Tirsdag

Claus wakes us at 7a.m. Eat breakfast at the Hotel Hafnia. Good Faroese yoghurt, rich and salty in taste, not so tart. Maybe interesting?

Meet with Johan Mortensen and 'the car dealer/man with the moustache' from Restorff Brewery in a local tavern. Listen to the stories and taste the beer from the brewery (one of the two in the Faroe Islands). Then go to the brewery for a tour. Meet the brewer in charge. Suggest an angelica beer. It does not arouse great interest. The two guys join us at the Hafnia for lunch. Buffet with a lot of boring stuff. Meet Martin Restorff, the director of the hotel. Together we plan a dinner for the following day with Faroese specialities. It will be in the hotel restaurant.

After lunch, we are driven to the ship Norôlysid. The skipper Birgir Enni, greets us with open arms. Fourteen years as skipper, and reportedly an excellent cook who dives for his shellfish, among others, hestemuslinger (Modiolus modiolus or horse mussel), like a giant clam that can live up to forty-five years and weigh up to 700 grams. We eat them raw, just as they are. A great taste of sea and 'meat'. The juice is very much like seawater in a creamy way. He also catches sea urchins from the seabed – best quality I have tasted. Not quite as intensely iodine-flavoured as in southern Europe. Large and meaty, sweet and very, very fresh.

Among the crew is Leif Sørensen, a trained chef from the restaurant Kommandanten in Copenhagen. He has brought the specialities skærpekød (air-cured mutton), restkød (cured lamb), tørfisk (dried fish) and saltet tørret grindevahl (salted dried pilot whale) for the four-hour boat trip around the Faroese archipelago. Incredibly beautiful journey sailing into sea caves. Leif tells us about fulmars. When the chicks are ready to fly their mothers push them off the rocks. But due to their heavy layer of blubber they cannot take off for the first few days, and therefore fall easy victim to fishing boats whose crews pull them in by the dozen. They are a great delicacy, but virtually impossible in Denmark, because the Faroese eat most of them.

We must try to get some home for a tasting. Leif's specialities were very interesting to foreigners. Very strong in flavour, salty, fermented, dried. I am not sure how the Danes will take to these flavours. One could possibly use them like spices. Birgir gave us some CDs of Faroese music recorded inside the sea caves. Evocative and soothing for the mind. Music in the restaurant?

After a boat trip with strong winds, we are once again on safe ground. It's a good thing we all took a sea sickness pill. The story goes that ships on their way from Iceland to Norway would be forced to leave those members of their crew who were suffering from sea sickness in the Faroe Islands. A nation is born.

Dinner at the Merlot restaurant. Spend time discussing tour own restaurant's name. Gultop, Blue, Frost, Freja, Havmost, etc. We have not come any closer. Quite the opposite. The chef prepares the horse mussels that we brought – boiled and baked. The taste was as we had expected, salty and very much like fish roe. The baked dish was considerably more elegant than the boiled one. This ingredient would be good smoked and possibly dried, and perhaps as a flan or soup or in a blended creamy texture. The raw ones we tasted on the boat earlier in the day were the best. For the next course we had fried lundelår (Fratercula arctica *or Atlantic puffin). They looked incredibly delicious, a little like confit of* vagtellår (Coturnix coturnix *or quail) legs. But we were quickly greeted by the foul odour of cod liver oil, and after having planted our teeth in this shoesole-tough meat, I am in no doubt that lundelår will not be on the menu in our restaurant. The main course was lamb from Iceland. Tender, good. The desserts were OK.*

11 p.m. Home again. Claus has seventy emails to reply to. He tries and tries again, but falls asleep over the computer. Mads goes to bed with Møllehave and René with Dostoevsky. Goodnight.

Onsdag

Get up at 8:30 a.m. Quick breakfast at the Hafnia. Arrive fifteen minutes late at Birgir Enni's Norôlysid. We are sailing to a salt cod factory (United Seafood). The weather is fantastic. The sun is shining and it is utterly calm. Now the Faroese land-and sea-scape are really beautiful.

At the factory we meet the director, Birgir Nonsgjogv. He shows us around and presents his products, salted cod, cod cheeks and cod tongues. The cod (66 kroner per kilo) is of the best quality and as fresh as possible. The finest fish from the area of sea that the Faroese call 'fôryn bank'. 'Deeper water, colder, more taste' says Birgir. His fish have been salted in brine for twenty hours, then salt-dried for eight days. The jaws (20 kroner per kilo) are sold with cheekbones, and there is therefore something like a 50 per cent loss. The tongues (65 kroner per kilo) only need the membrane removed so there is little loss. Tongues and cheeks are sold in 10kg pails in a 20 per cent salt brine. He uses phosphate in the salt! Almost all his fish are sold to Spain.

We drive out to another factory (Faroe Marine Products), where the smell is so foul that any normal person would retreat in disgust. We stay for one hour. The managing director meets us at the entrance, and introduces himself as Eirikur â Husamørk. The factory only dries fish heads (30 kroner per kilo), and lots of them. Mainly cod but also other fish varieties. Oddly enough, 95 per cent of the production is sold to Nigeria. They use the heads their for special occasions. The drying takes one to two weeks, and the heads are then packed in 30kg sacks. They are apparently fantastic for soups.

Back to Tórshavn fast. We are already half an hour late for our next meeting, with the great artist Trôndur Pattursson. Taxi to Kirkebø with a quick stop at the baker's to get drilur *(a type of dark rye bread)... Tastes great, will be used at the restaurant in one way or another.*

Trôndur's house is a fantastic place. Everything is built in driftwood and stone. Located 30 metres up on a hill as close to the water as you can get. The silence is deep, the air is clean and the presence of nature is overwhelming. As we drink beer with Trôndur, we listen to his wild stories and suggestions for the restaurant's name. We see his family farm and feel 'the Viking spirit' in the 900-year-old dining hall. Trôndur explains that everything in the dining room is original. It's difficult to believe that you can find something so old and authentic in the West, and that it's still inhabited. It's almost like standing in the middle of a film set. This I will never forget! We meet his nephew, Joannes Patursson, who is a farmer and breeds lambs, supreme quality. The animals live on the wild grasses that grow on his land – all completely natural! May be able to buy lamb from him in the right season. But it may be difficult to import it into Denmark, as the Faroese don't have an EU-sanctioned abattoir.

On the way back to Tórshavn, we make a stop at Eydun's. He shows us his work in basalt. We make arrangements for him to try to drill an indentation on a small fragment. Perhaps to be used in the restaurant as a plate. Stone should be a significant material in the restaurant. Trôndur drives us to the Hotel Hafnia, where we eat an eight-course menu with Faroese specialities. Marinated raw whale, puffin, angler fish, cod jaw, whale steak with fried onions, fulmar, rhubarb. I guess the meal could be described as 'interesting'.

The puffin was good raw – creamy with an understated taste of sea. However, when cooked it develops a light flavour of cod liver oil. How odd! During the cheese, our new friend Birgir Enni arrived. Claus went to the toilet and fell asleep, believe it or not – and it was a very small toilet, no bigger than a school lavatory. It's one o'clock. We should have been in bed an hour ago.

Torsdag

Again up too late! Hurry down to the tourist office to book a car. The time is 9.40 a.m. We have to be in Leirvik at 11 a.m. or we won't make the ferry to Klaksvik, the second largest city of the Faroe Islands with approximately 5,000 inhabitants. A taxi to the baker's to get drilur, *and then on to the car rental office. We get to the port at 10.58 a.m.*

Unbelievably beautiful approach to the port at Klaksvik (according to our guidebook, the most beautiful approach in the world). A totally windless, sunny day again. Drive directly to the Föroya Bjór brewery. Einar Waag, managing director and third generation at Föroya Bjór, welcomes us. Very hospitable people. Lunch and conversation at Einar's. Then a tour of the brewery. The beer tastes great! 'Black Sheep' especially packs a punch. Perhaps we could use their gold or strong beer?

On the way home we stop in Leynar, at the house of Ole Jacob Nielsen, an artist-craftsman in wood. A really charming, happy person, he offers beer. We hear about the uncompromising way he uses his materials. He only uses Faroese wood, and always lets its natural shape and structure dictate the appearance of the piece. Therefore each is unique. In the end, we stay for three hours. We see his workshop and gallery. The wood is comfortably soft and smooth to the touch. You almost feel that it breathes softly in your hand when you touch it. We commission him to make the salt jars for the restaurant. Small fine salt jars made from the root of a rowan that he found after a fierce autumn storm had uprooted some fully grown bushes. It is illegal to chop down the few 'trees' and bushes that grow on the Faroe Islands. Home again. Music from the 'caves'. Mads prepares salt cod with root vegetables, and after the fish we drink a 1985 amarone. Goodnight.

Fredag

Get up at 8.30 a.m. A very short programme for today. At 3.30 p.m. we shall be taking off for Iceland. Quiet and peaceful breakfast at the Hafnia. Short walk around town. We buy Faroese jumpers (sweaters).

We have a meeting at 11 a.m. with ceramicist Gurri Poulsen. Gurri, a lovely lady, welcomes us in her small workshop. Very beautiful ceramics, especially her tiles and teapots. She invites us to the Faroese Exhibition in Copenhagen at the end of the month. We arrange that she will probably make the teapots for the restaurant. Taxi to the airport.

The Faroe Islands have been a surprise. Friendly, helpful people. High-quality ingredients, sometimes unique. Not since I was in Macedonia have I been in a country where the original spirit and mood are preserved so intact. People live quietly and peacefully with nature – this is in fact all they can do, because nature is all around them. Thank you, Faroe Islands!

As we fly over the North Atlantic, our expectations are high, even if I don't know much about Iceland, beyond the fact that that around two hundred thousand people live on the huge volcanic island of the world-famous sagas. The plane is delayed, so we land in Reykjavik an hour later than expected. Taxi to the Radisson Saga Hotel, where we meet trade councillor Jon Åbergesson and his colleague Erna Bjornsdottir. A little surprise: our reservations have been cancelled, except for Claus's. We therefore stay with Edda and Sverrir. Edda is a set designer and Sverrir an opera singer. Their charming house is located in the centre of the old city. Inside, Icelandic art hangs everywhere. Edda and Sverrir seem very open and generous. Thank you, Radisson, for overbooking the hotel. We throw the suitcases down and Jon gives us a little tour around town. We taste the local 'hot dogs', made of lamb and Icelandic beer. Good, but I'm not much into hot dogs, and Icelanders don't change my mind.

Back to the house. Our hosts treat us to a cup of tea at the newly opened sushi bar around the corner. Cosy, very hospitable and surprising. Jon takes us for dinner at Vid Tjornina, a classical fish restaurant, which has been running for twenty years. It's actually a large second-floor apartment, measuring 200 – 300 square metres. The original rooms have been divided into a lounge and little private rooms. The actual living room/dining room functions as an à la carte restaurant. The menu started with a ceviche of three types of seafood: salmon, scallops and halibut. The second course was fish soup with haddock. The third course was torskekinder *(cod's cheek) with a chive sauce. The main course was halibut with spinach and potatoes. The meal was good, more universally European than ethnic Icelandic. The fish was super high-quality. The halibut unique. Shellfish from the Faroe Islands, fish from Iceland? We skipped dessert as we were very tired. Finished the day with a warm sake at the sushi bar to wind down.* Goodnight.

Lørdag

Get up at 9 a.m. Eat breakfast with Edda and Sverrir. We taste Sverrir's home-made tea, from an old Viking recipe of organic dried spices and herbs. Wow! Maybe he will blend it for the restaurant or let us know the mixture? We hear about their friends in the art business and they give us tips on which galleries, artists and ceramicists we should visit. Among other things, we are invited to the opening of an exhibition of work by the eighty-five-year-old wood artist Sæmundur Valdimarsson.

We meet up with Claus and Erna. Today we will visit ceramicists, artists, etc. We start with ceramicist Kolbrún Björgólfsdottir, who among other things has created some beautiful egg cups with runes carved on the side. They would be great for snacks. Except for that, there was nothing of interest. We arrange to meet again on Monday or Tuesday.

Valdis Harrysdottir is next. She belongs to a small group of ten artists who run a gallery. She creates small bowls in papier mâché, on which are glued dried slices of fruit and vegetable. Some of them would be perfect for snacks. The only problem is that they are very porous and do not tolerate too much fat or moisture. We agree to come back in the next few days. We meet other artists – lots of beautiful things, but nothing that fits into the restaurant.

At 2 p.m. Mads and I are at the preview of Sæmundur Valdimarsson's work, which is absolutely fantastic. We are particularly impressed by one piece. Dark wood and blue hair, neither woman nor man, perhaps an elf, but certainly a child of Iceland.

After the preview, Sverrir drives us to the bus to take us to the Blue Lagoon. Entering the lagoon, we meet Claus, who is on his way home. He wants to watch the football (Iceland vs Germany, 0–0). The Blue Lagoon is something you must see with your own eyes. In the middle of the lava landscape, a good hour's ride from Reykjavik, large vapour clouds suddenly appear. Hot springs that you would otherwise be able to boil vegetables in are computer-controlled to perfect bathing temperatures. If you can live with the sulphurous smell, which is at times powerful, it is easy to spend a day in this place.

Dinner is at the restaurant of Siggi Hall, probably Iceland's best-known chef. Erna is our host. I know Eythor, the chef de cuisine. He was employed as a chef at Kong Hans Kælder, in Copenhagen.

Eythor puts together a five-course meal for us. Appetizer: crisp roll with reindeer rillette. Starter: cod with a pepper marmalade and brown butter. Middle course: fried breaded halibut with løjrogn (roe). The løjrogn is very tasty, super-fresh and completely yellow here in Iceland, not like we know it at home in Denmark, with added colourant and salt, and without taste. A great discovery that I can and shall use. Second 'middle course' fried, salted cod with pickled garlic and spinach. Main course: reindeer and lamb cutlets with pommes Anna. The reindeer was delicious – it was the first time I had tasted it. Super-tender, juicy and slightly sweet. There was perhaps a little iron in the taste, which could put some people off. Otherwise, it's another product I can and shall use. The Icelandic lamb is very tender, and not as tough and wooly in flavour as the Danish. The best meat, according to the locals and Siggi, comes from the northern part of the island. We arrange to meet Siggi later in the week. He would like to help us make contacts.

The dessert – chocolate fondant with cardamom ice-cream and crème brûlée with strawberries and almond cake. A cup of coffee. We stay and wait for Eythor. Drink a few beers in town and get to bed a little too late. The rumours of Iceland's nightlife are confirmed. Goodnight.

Søndag

Get up at 9 a.m. and eat breakfast with Edda outside on their terrace. I taste the tea again. Wow! Fetched by Lara Hana (our driver for the day). We don't have a big programme for today as it is Sunday and everywhere 'official' is closed. The plans are to see the Gyldenfoss waterfall, and a huge geyser. We will be tourists for today.

Gyldenfoss is enormous – icy-cold water from one of the great glaciers thrown against the lava rocks. The forces of nature at their most impressive. We climb on to the rocks around the waterfall. We find Icelandic wild thyme or Skotsk timian (Scottish thyme). The taste is very strong and intense, a mild lemon aftertaste – fantastic! We will explore wild plants a lot.

After lunch we drive to the geyser, which is the biggest of its kind in the

North. A geyser is a hot spring that rises from 30 metres below ground, where it lies close to the liquid and incredibly hot magma rock. The magma causes the water to evaporate into high-pressure steam, which then shoots up to the surface and rises 20 metres into the air. Wild! Drive home again. Have to meet Sveinn Björnsson, a representative from the Foreign Ministry, for dinner. Get picked up by Sveinn and his wife. It seemed like they were indifferent to everything about the project – a mere official business commitment to them – but I could be wrong. You might call him a little arrogant. For instance, he said at one point that Danes don't like lamb because they have bad taste! But dinner went well at the Vio Fjorubordid restaurant. The menu consisted of langoustine soup for starter, and boiled langoustine for main course. The langoustines were not of the best quality – not too firm and a little muddy in flavour. The restaurant uses 250 kilos of frozen tails a week. Will have to taste them fresh before they are written off. Drive home to bed. Goodnight.

Mandag

Early start, breakfast with Sverrir and Edda. I drink four mugs of tea. At eight o'clock Erna picks us up and we drive to a little shop that dries fish. Not an interesting place – only stay for five minutes. Move on to Erna's office to plan the rest of the day.

The day's second visit is to Egils, one of the breweries in Iceland that also makes an Icelandic vodka. The beer is good, particularly the golden beer. The malt soda was also delicious – deep and with a clear and good flavour of malt. We taste a barrel-aged luxury brennivin (aquavit), deliciously round palate with a mild sweetness from the oak. We taste the vodka, 45 per cent, triple distilled – a good hot and tasty vodka! Next stop is an organic bakery – delicious bread with a good crispy crust. But all the bread was Italian-style, and there were no 'classic' breads baked by old-fashioned methods or following any particularly Icelandic recipes. The garlic bread was the best, but not anything we would use.

Afterwards we paid a visit to one of the best fishmongers – this at least is what we were told – which turned out to be a type of fish 'deli-takeaway'. A place where the fish are prepared with different marinades and dry or fresh herbs. There were also plokkfiskur (fish salads), haddock boiled with potatoes, mashed with lots of butter and onion. The idea is that you take home the marinated fish and prepare it. Not a product we would be able to use, but the idea was super. We did taste a really good smoked trout. Not too fat, and with a really good smoky flavour. We got the name of the supplier (Reykas smokehouse), and perhaps later we can hear the secret behind the smoking methods of this place.

Ten minutes later we arrived at an organic dairy, Bio-bú, where we met Susanne Freuler, the laboratory technician there. The products were more or less just thin yoghurt. Not interesting. The dairy had only just started up and this is why there weren't many products. Perhaps at a later stage there will be butter, so we agreed to meet again when the butter is available. Apparently Icelandic cows are a completely pure breed, which can be traced back to Viking times. They are free-range, and produce about half the milk of a Danish cow. Extra high-quality? We'll have to taste more dairy products from Iceland.

Lunch at Hotel Nordica. We meet the head chef, Hákon Már Örvarsson, and his right-hand man Günner, who has worked at Komandanten in Copenhagen. They were both very helpful and friendly. Will keep in touch with them when back home in Denmark. There were also three other guys present: Hördur Sigurgestsson, the hotel's managing director; Þorsteinn Gunnarsson, CEO of Icelandair; and Gudmundur' Arnason, head of the Education Ministry. We had a very nice lunch starting with raw marinated veal with different salads. For main course you could choose between cod with asparagus, and salmon and langoustine parcels. Dessert was a free-choice buffet. Hákon and Günner showed us around the huge kitchen – millions had been spent on the kitchen and appliances, everything is the newest of the new, ovens, fridges, stove, yes, everything. It's obvious that the Icelanders really want to be ahead of the game in terms of food. We say a friendly goodbye and hurry on to the next stop.

We meet with Einar Matthiasson at the MS dairy. He has organized a tasting of their skyr. Skyr is a cottage-type cheese with deep roots in Icelandic history that can be traced back a thousand years, and the recipe hasn't really changed since! Wild! The milk is heated, then cooled to 40°C. You add rennet and old skyr. It matures for a full day in a muslin (cheesecloth). Then it can be mixed as you like it – with milk or cream – and you can use it in pastries, desserts, etc. Skyr just tastes damn good: creamy, low-fat and with a very deep flavour, much better than fromage blanc. Perhaps the special milk from the indigenous cows really makes a difference? Another product we must use: the whey which is sieved out is called mysa. In the old days they used mysa to marinate and conserve meat. It is very acidic and has an animal hint in its flavour. It actually tastes quite good and could perhaps replace lemon juice or white wine in sauces or vinaigrettes. There are two variations: drinking mysa or acid mysa—the only difference being that the acid mysa is more acidic.

We make a quick stop at a fur shop. Architect Signe would like some samples of fish skins and lamb hides.

Quickly home and change into a shirt. We are meeting the former President of Iceland, Vigdís Finnbogadóttir. She has invited us to her summerhouse by the Great Lake, the largest in Iceland. The area is incredibly beautiful. Everything feels untouched: the clear, delicious water in the rivers, the gentle hills and the huge rocks. It was a great experience! We swim with the fish in the cold water. Vigdís offers brennivin and beer while she shows us around her house, which faces Tingvellei. She is a very gentle and good person. She seems generous and intelligent, and has fantastic charisma.

In the evening, we all drive back to town. Gudmundur Arnason is waiting for us in De Tre Franskmænd (The Three Frenchmen), one of the city's oldest fish restaurants. We eat raw whale and raw cold-smoked puffin. It tastes really good – much better than in the Faroe Islands, and again a fantastic halibut, also the quality of the flounder is particularly superior. Jon follows us home, and says goodbye. Goodnight.

Tirsdag

Claus returns to Copenhagen at 11 a.m. Start the day with a breakfast meeting at the Hotel Saga with Karl Sølmunarson from the Tros fish factory, which is the best exporter of fresh fish. The meeting is extremely constructive, and we believe we have made a good contact. Now we just need some good flight prices from Icelandair. The fresh fish here in Iceland is among the best I have tasted.

We quickly move on to Reykas smokehouse, whose top-notch product we tasted the previous day at the fish deli. They buy wild salmon and trout from local fishermen. Private individuals can also bring their fish to be smoked. The smoking method is quite standard, with beech as the smoking wood. We make a stop at one of the big dairies to taste butter and cheese. They were good products, but we believe that we can get better from the small dairies at home.

Mads and I stop at Kristin's, to talk about Icelandic art and culture with this well-known artist. We order eight snack containers at Kogga's and eight petit four holders from Gudrid Poulsen, a ceramicist we met the same day.

In the evening we briefly meet Siggi Hall to say goodbye. He is clearly the man who can make things happen in Iceland. Charming, keep in

*touch. Then we eat sushi to taste some raw fish, drink some green tea
and go to bed.* Goodnight.

Onsdag

*Get up early. At 7.15 a.m. we leave for Greenland. Eat breakfast with Sverrir
and Edda, and arrange for Sverriir to make some kind of medieval mixture
for us. His tea tastes so good. We exchange addresses and get driven to the
airport. Sverrir and Edda are some of the friendliest and most loving people
we have met in Iceland. We will see a lot more of them.*

*Iceland has been markedly different from the Faroe Islands. The common
denominator of the two countries is untouched nature, a great sense of space
and beautiful settings, which I haven't experienced elsewhere. But Iceland feels
a lot more like mainland Europe – there is a great energy and you feel that its
citizens want to get ahead in the world. Super-modern society. The Icelanders
we met also have a sense of detail. Their ceramics were modern with a
reference to something original. Everywhere we seemed to meet creative
people who are constantly planning ahead. This energy I shall bring back
to Denmark along with the skyr, cod, halibut and roe. Thank you, Iceland.*

*Departure from Reykjavik at 10.45 a.m. for arrival in Narsarsuaq, southern
Greenland. The worst flight ever. The landing is through a fjord enclosed by
mountains. There were strong gusts of wind that constantly changed from
one cliff to another. These winds were leftovers from an American hurricane.
It was so bad that at one point I thought it was the end, and that we were
going down. There was an older lady next to me who was praying with folded
hands. A bad experience. Greeted at the airport by Poul Erik Pedersen, a
strange companion with a US cap and a lumberjack jacket. Very quiet, with
large, coarse hands, almost larger than the rifle he has with him. Strange day
so far! Erik will take us by boat to Narssaq, a trip of a couple of hours. The boat
ride was a bizarre experience. But perhaps I'm too conventional – perhaps
it's normal to slalom between deep blue ice floes in a rebellious sea. In a way,
incredibly beautiful and unique, but also very unpleasant.*

*At the quay in Narssaq, Morten Mikkelsen picks us up. He's a chef and
teacher at Inuilli, the only cookery school in Greenland, which will be our
home in Narssaq. It's almost impossible to think of a more perfect spot for
the school. From our window we have a view of great fragments of ice floes
that float lazily in the clear blue sea. Small, soft, flower-covered hills
everywhere. How lucky we are!*

The school experiments with Greenlandic ingredients. The students collect wild herbs and berries from the moors. We taste rosenrod *(Rhodiola rosea or golden root or roseroot), a plant that grows by the water. Very aromatic, its root is supposedly good dry. Also* klokkeblomst, *a member of the bellflower family or* Campanulaceae, *a fantastically sweet flower that grows on the moors, very tasty, possibly to be used in vinegars, parfaits and marinades, sprinkled over a piece of cooked wild meat, etc. Also Greenlandic post, a herb that can resemble rosemary or marjoram. Wow! The* Skotsk timian *is more powerful and tart than the thyme we know, though not quite as citrussy as the Icelandic. There are also blueberries, blackberries and* tyttebær (Vaccinium vitis-idaea *or cowberry) like we have never tasted before. Wild berries we will use in abundance if I can get them of this quality. Wild kvan* (Angelica sylvestris *or angelica) has an almost violent flavour. We try some shoots and they taste like a cross between celery and lovage. The school is a unique place and seems better than its Danish 'sister'. Everything is home-made, from charcuterie to sweet angelica crisps. So cool that they explore their own produce.*

We meet Rie Oldenburg, museum director and author of a book on Greenlandic cuisine (she gives us a copy). We spend an hour at her house, where we talk about the cultural history of food in Greenland. Hurry home. Denmark is playing an international football match. As usual Denmark plays really badly, but it's a draw at the last minute.

Dinner at the school. Some of the students make and serve food for us. This they do every day for each other. This is unusual for a school of its kind. The Wiener schnitzel tastes good! René beats Mads at table tennis. We drink a glass of wine with a couple of the locals. Unusual but good day. Goodnight.

Torsdag

Get up at 8 a.m., eat breakfast at the school's restaurant, everything home-made – how cool is this to see? Have a short morning meeting with the school principal, Esben Toftdahl, and Morten. We will try to set up some kind of collaboration and possibly take a couple of their students a year. In return, they will collect wild herbs and berries in season for us. The great problem is getting them to Denmark while still fresh. Have to find a solution. Possibly we could dry them. It is also a possibility to have them transported frozen. Takes around two weeks. Approximate price as freight on ferries is 50 Dkr. We will have to look around our own neighbourhood in Copenhagen to see if we can find similar ingredients. We go for a quick walk into town to see what the locals call brættet – *the board. It's a place where the local fishermen and hunters can sell the catch of the day – anything from seagulls to whale meat to porpoise. Today there was freshly caught seal, seagulls, cod, catfish and lots of berries, flowers and roots from the moors.* Brættet *in a small town in southern Greenland is better than our market (Israels Plads) back home in Denmark. We get driven to the harbour, where a ship called* Sarpik Ittuk *awaits us. Ahead of us are two days of sailing to Nuuk. We pray for good weather, while we swallow a handful of seasickness pills.*

There's not much to do on the ship, so I have a lot of time to reflect on the past ten days. We sit on deck wrapped in five layers of clothing and fall asleep to the rocking of the ship, the crisp, clean air and the ringing silence. Wake when the ship docks in Julianehåb, where we spend two hours. We see the city and meet Poul Erik Pedersen on his bicycle. He lives here in town. We chat a little about the wind and weather. In all three countries it has been fairly easy to communicate with people. We do a bit of shopping for snacks and eat warm fishcakes for lunch.

Read a little in the cabin, have almost finished Crime and Punishment. *Try to fall asleep when a storm is brewing and the waves slowly growing larger. Fall asleep. Get woken a couple of hours later by the captain with an announcement that there is an extremely powerful display of Northern Light. Aurora borealis! On many occasions when I worked as a waiter I talked to tourists about the Northern Lights. Many asked me about them. I did not understand the fascination. I had seen a photo, but I thought it could not justify a trip so far up north. It is difficult to describe how beautiful it really is. A photograph cannot match the magic in the changing colours, the soft dancing tones in the clouds. I wish I had the ability to do it justice with words. Unfortunately I cannot. But I would gladly go to Greenland, fly through a small hurricane and sail through monstrous waves to relive the ten minutes of magic I experienced here.* Goodnight.

Fredag

Sleep in, mainly due to the wild rolling of the boat. Do not make it for breakfast. The restaurant is open for one hour in the morning and one in the evening. Otherwise there is only water, beer and candy in the shop. Mads eats Toblerone for breakfast and I eat digestive biscuits. Have a shower. Try to get out on deck but the wind is too strong and the fog too dense. Mads sleeps again. I read.

Sleep through lunch. Eat apple, share a cucumber and a packet of caramel-flavoured digestive biscuits. Two o'clock. The wind has dropped and the fog has burnt off. We lie on deck, enjoy the sun, the silence, the air and nature. All around the ship are mountains covered in snow and huge slabs of granite. It is as if time stands still here. Everything is so unspoilt. Here nothing comes easily. Nature rules.

At 5.30 p.m. everyone on the boat queues up for dinner. The menu: asparagus soup, old-fashioned roast beef with gravy, vanilla mousse. It does not taste good! Arrive in Nuuk at 9.30 p.m. Hanne, the mother-in-law of our tour operator from Copenhagen, Aviaja, is waiting on a pier with a small sign on which she has neatly written 'Mads and René'. We drive back to her house to go over the programme and get a little bite to eat. We check our email for the first time in two days. The mood turns sour when we read the news from Signe, our architect. Once again there are problems with the grant. But the mood quickly changes when Hanne pours a glass of wine. We just chat for an hour. Among other things she will try to set up a meeting with Michael Binzer, marketing director for Air Greenland. She will also try to get us on the radio! Around midnight we check in at Hotel Nuuk. Finally a hotel room. Listen to a little music. Goodnight.

Lørdag

Get up at 8 a.m. and eat breakfast. Ring Titus Lennert, Aviaja's uncle. He will be our guide for part of the day. We drive down to Brættet. There is a lot of meat, especially reindeer as the season has just started. Oddly enough there is not much fresh fish, only a little cod, catfish and salmon (Titus tells us that Greenlanders are generally a meat-eating people whenever possible). We shop for a little heather-smoked wild trout and dried reindeer for lunch. We get a brief tour of the town and then meet his wife for lunch. Mads does not like the dried reindeer meat. The flavour of iron is too strong. I quite like it but it truly does taste a lot of iron. Just like fried liver does – and I love that. It is possibly a little too unusual for most palates. Perhaps it can be used as a spice? However, we both agree that the fish has been too strongly smoked. The flavour has become a little metallic, but the fish is of good quality.

After lunch we arrange on the telephone to go to the house of Julie Hardenberg, who is having a little party tonight. Julie is among other things a photographic artist and writer who has recently published a children's book in Greenlandic. We hurry home to get a shower, buying *a bottle of wine on the way (395 Dkr), then leave for dinner. The atmosphere is good and very relaxed, the guests ranging from artists to geologists to film-makers to craftspeople. Everyone has brought something to eat. There is porpoise soup, which tastes a little like roast beef in a dry way, but good. Slowly cooked reindeer leg, really tasty, and classical European dishes: pasta salad, potato salad, couscous. We hold a little competition for the name of the restaurant. Everyone has fifteen minutes to think of a name that sums up the North. It must have an international quality, not too ethnic Nordic, and it may come from something traditional, but it's very important that it also looks forward to the future. This was the brief before the competition. Everyone really went for it and we had many good suggestions. The winner was 'Avala'. 'Avala' means motion, to take on new challenges. Not bad. We strike up a conversation with one of the guests who is a geologist. He tells us of basalt, about how it develops in the centre of the earth, and that in a way it's the foundation for the North Atlantic. Actually Iceland, the Faroe Islands and the Disko Islands are ninety per cent basalt. After having spoken to him we are no longer in doubt that the restaurant will be called Basalt. We only have to convince the others of it.*

We also meet Poul E Jensen, who, besides being the clown of the evening, is working on a very exciting mineral water. The stream runs straight out of Nuuk and the water should be extremely clean and tasty. The unusual thing is that the source is deep within the earth and therefore the water is at a constant temperature of 35°C. This means that it is accessible all year, unlike other sources in Greenland that freeze in winter.

We decided not to leave too late because we will be meeting Rune, the owner of Greenland's best restaurant, Nipisa, early tomorrow morning. Super-nice evening, with friendly people. Goodnight.

Søndag

Picked up at 10 a.m. by Rune. We are going sailing. The weather is perfect, with a dead-calm sea and the mild air. We hope to spot humpback whales, possibly also seals.

After nearly fifteen minutes of sailing, we see the first whales. Rune speeds to catch up and we quickly get close to them. We spend the next hour and a half with the whales, seeing these 35-ton mammals so close that we can almost touch them. At one moment we even felt their spout, which actually wasn't such a great experience. The best way to describe it is like bad breath. It was the first time I had seen a whale, and then to experience them so closely! How lucky are we – I could have spent all day and evening with them! We eat lunch, brought by Rune, at sea: Greenlandic lamb, fried reindeer, smoked whale, fried puffin, smoked halibut and salmon terrine, musk sausage and raw prawns. Everything was delicious, especially the raw prawns. Sweet and very tasty, with the consistency of soft butter. Some of these prawns will be coming back for the restaurant. After lunch we suddenly spot seals, and in no time Rune has his gun loaded – the hunt has begun. After an hour's chase, and one shot fired unsuccessfully, we give up and sail back to port. Before we say goodbye we reserve a table at the restaurant for Monday evening.

Our next stop is to see Lars Rosing, a local carpenter whom we met at Julie Hardenberg's party. We drive to the house of his older brother Michael, a biologist and also an amateur maker of snaps. He has made everything into snaps: angelica, rosenrod, rødknae (Rumex acetosella or sheep sorrel), crowberry, post, thyme, mosebær, rypekro. Rypekro snaps taste fantastic, and they were actually the reason for our visit.

The rype (Lagopus lagopus scoticus or red grouse) is a vegetarian gamebird, which feeds mainly on plant buds, but also on berries when in season. These buds and berries drop into a small sac under the beak where leaves and twigs are sieved out and slight fermentation takes place. When hunters shoot the birds they save the kro, as this green, moist substance is called, and use it for snaps. There is a great difference in how kro tastes, depending on the season and what is available to eat. But it is very unusual in an interesting way. We must be able to use it for other things than snaps: sauces, dried as spice and infused into oils. The children of Greenland blow up the empty sac like a tiny ballon. We brought a little kro back and arranged for Michael to get us 4 – 5 kilos every year.

We have a free evening and eat a light supper at a local restaurant while we give an interview on the radio. Go home and read. Early to bed, completely tired. The boat trip drained our strength, strangely enough. Goodnight.

PORTRAIT
OF A
NORDIC
CHEF

Rune Skyum-Nielsen

When René Redzepi was a boy, there was absolutely no indication that he would one day be considered as one of the most visionary chefs in the world of international gastronomy. If anyone was destined to go far it was more likely to be his twin brother, Kenneth. While Kenneth was diligent and studious, René hated sitting still in lessons. Although his bilingual upbringing – his father was from Macedonia, his mother from Copenhagen – equipped him with an aptitude for English and French, René quickly developed into one of the troublemakers in his primary school on the outskirts of a working-class district of Copenhagen. He was, quite simply, a short, stocky, excitable lad with Balkan blood coursing through his veins, who had a tendency to fall asleep when lessons were boring. However, René and Kenneth had one thing in common: the will to work hard. When they were only nine years old, the Redzepi brothers were a topic of conversation at the offices of the local weekly paper. Young lads doing ten newspaper delivery rounds each on Wednesdays and Saturdays commanded respect. 'In January the sales adverts were so bulky that the piles of newspapers were taller than we were', René recalls. But that wasn't all. The brothers also wobbled out on errands for the man who ran the kiosk on the corner. He provided a delivery bicycle that was far too big for them, and paid them five crowns for each crate of beer they delivered. And finally, the brothers were 'bottle boys' for a nearby supermarket.

Their father and mother worked respectively as a taxi driver and a cleaner, and the twins had to pay for their own clothes, camping trips and membership of various handball and basketball clubs. When summer arrived, the family would travel south by bus to their father's old home in Macedonia. They would stay there for three to six months at a time, and the twins would be taught by their mother so that they wouldn't fall behind at school. The standard of living in Macedonia was modest, and a degree of adjustment was needed on arrival after spending the rest of the year in prosperous Scandinavia. For years there were only two cars driving around the scorched local streets, and if the boys were going to visit an aunt who lived some distance away they went by horse and cart. The grown-ups spent their days in the fields, while the youngsters ran around on the nearby mountainsides, picking wild blackberries and collecting chestnuts. If it was going to be chicken for supper, the family killed the bird themselves. If they needed milk, they milked the cows. If they needed butter for their bread, they baked first and then churned the butter. René was a reluctant participant in these daily chores and didn't like helping in the poorly equipped kitchen of his Macedonian relatives. 'Most of all, I thought it was embarrassing to go back to school in Denmark when summer was over and talk about how we ate sitting cross-legged on the floor.'

René's family had a rather different approach to cooking from that of the average Danish family, who in those days, the 1980s, resorted to the big selection of frozen food and ready-prepared meals in the supermarkets. 'When all the others were getting fish fingers, fig spread and chicken for Saturday lunch, we didn't have the money for much of that kind of thing. Instead our parents prepared sliced tomatoes with vinegar, salt and olive oil or chicken livers and butter beans. That's the kind of thing I grew up with.'

When they were leaving school one of René's friends applied to restaurant school, and as René didn't have anything better to do he went too. Not that he had ever dreamt of going down that route. After a couple of days the teacher arranged a food competition, and it was decisive for his future. René and his friend scanned the available recipe books and chose chicken with cashew nut sauce. 'I had never heard of cashew nuts before and I thought it would impress the teacher. When it was time to serve the dish my friend wanted to pour the sauce over the chicken, but I said, "No, no, you should be able to see everything." That competition was a landmark for me. I felt different about myself. I was fifteen years old, and usually what I was most worried about was whether I was going to play football that day or not. But quite suddenly I had to decide what it was I liked about food, what I wanted to show the others, and how I would go about winning that competition… I was hooked', René recalls.

After a year at the restaurant school, he had to go out and find an apprenticeship. The sixteen-year-old received a couple of sharp rebuffs, so made do with a place as a trainee waiter at the Palads Hotel. Not until three years later, in 1996, did a Copenhagen Michelin restaurant, the family-run Pierre André, take pity on René and accept him. The chef, Philippe Houdet, had so much confidence in René that during the last part of his three years' apprenticeship he was allowed to influence the menu – with, among other things, a rather exotic combination of caramelized chicory and lemon sorbet, a dish that could never be considered at Noma today.

In 1998, when René had become interested in going abroad, Philippe Houdet didn't hesitate to fax off testimonials. Eight minutes later a fax came back from Le Jardin des Sens – the Garden of the Senses in Montpellier in southern France. This restaurant, which had been decorated with the almost unattainable three Michelin stars, would be pleased to employ the Dane over the summer. A dream had come true for René Redzepi – the first of many. After that, of course, he extended his experience in various countries, in the kitchens of elBulli, the French Laundry and the Kong Hans, among others, before embarking on the Noma venture.

In 2008 René Redzepi became a father for the first time, when his wife Nadine, gave birth to their daughter, Arwen. This new responsibility has restricted his opportunities and his desire to go off on long stays abroad, but he is hungry for knowledge and still occasionally goes away to learn something new. For example, he spent two weeks as an ordinary cook at a three-star restaurant in the Japanese city of Kyoto in December 2009. Two months later he went back to Iceland, where he had set himself the task of investigating what effect this North Atlantic country's financial roller-coaster ride might have on Icelandic cuisine. On the way he came across a number of interesting taste experiences: bread baked over a lava source, sea cucumbers and sea urchins, new types of seaweed and even horsemeat.

'When you can no longer afford to import raw materials, you automatically look to see what you have yourself that you can do something with and how you can be self-sufficient. Hopefully it will be good for the Icelanders' cuisine in the long term, and reintroduce the rich selections of fish that were their everyday fare just ten or twenty years ago', comments René.

In addition, about once a month he travels abroad to take part in workshops and conferences with other top international chefs. The culinary acrobats of his generation differ in many ways from their predecessors because they don't just compete with one another, they also cooperate. So in May 2009, when Noma acted as host for a summit meeting of twelve international chefs with a great future before them, it was to learn from one another and to see the different ways in which they went about things. This random collection of talents included among others Claude Bosi, David Chang, Pascal Barbot, Albert Adrià, Inaki Aizpitarte, Ichiro Kubuta, Wylie Dufresne and Daniel Patterson.

'At such meetings, I invite the personalities who have the sharpest profile and who work wholeheartedly on their projects,' explains René. 'They are all people I have heard of, read about or met before. Experiences like this give a great boost to all aspects of Noma's quality, because we are allowed to see and experience gifted people with widely differing backgrounds tackling the same tasks each in their individual ways.' René dismisses the idea that there would be anything other than healthy competition among the new elite on the gastronomic scene. 'Inspiration is only something healthy. No one steals anyone else's ideas. And anyway, how could we do that and keep our own vision intact?'

If, like René, you spend by far the greatest part of your waking hours at work, it is perhaps not surprising that that is where he met his wife, Nadine. She was one of the waitresses, and he was single again after a long-lasting relationship which had fallen victim to his working week of eighty or ninety hours. For the time being, the couple are planning to prioritize Nordic cuisine for the next ten years – minimum. 'Until then we will consider the situation. The project has already taken so many twists and turns. We have gone from being the joke of the town to being the gastronomic traveller's first impression of Danish food. It's an incredible responsibility. Noma has broken through the barrier in Germany, where information from Scandinavia usually stops. We have to exploit this. And becoming a father means first and foremost that I will work even harder to make Noma a success. That may sound like a cliché, but I would like to think that my children will not have to slave nearly as hard as I have.'

TIME
AND
PLACE

Photographs by
Ditte Isager

Photographs styled by
Christine Rudolph

WHITE CURRANTS

White currants have a sharp, astringent taste, and are a perfect accompaniment to shellfish, unlike their sweeter cousin, the red currant.

56

ONIONS

Onions from Læsø, where a variety indigenous to the Danish island still grow.

57

CARAMEL
AND
MALT

58 (257)

BOUILLON
OF
STEAMED BIRCHWOOD, CHANTERELLES
AND
FRESH HAZELNUT

59 (258)

BIRCH FOREST

A forest of birch trees near the home of Tage Rønne.

60

FRESH LEEKS

61

ASPARAGUS, BULRUSH
AND
DUCK EGGS

62 (259)

AEBLESKIVER
AND
VINEGAR MERINGUES

63 (260)

WHITE CURRANTS
AND
GELLED CUCUMBER JUICE, SWEET CICELY
AND
HAZELNUT MILK

64 (261)

POTATO CRISPS
AND
YOGHURT

65 (262)

CLOUDBERRIES
FROM
PITEÅ, BURNT MERINGUE
AND
HERBAL TEA

66 (263)

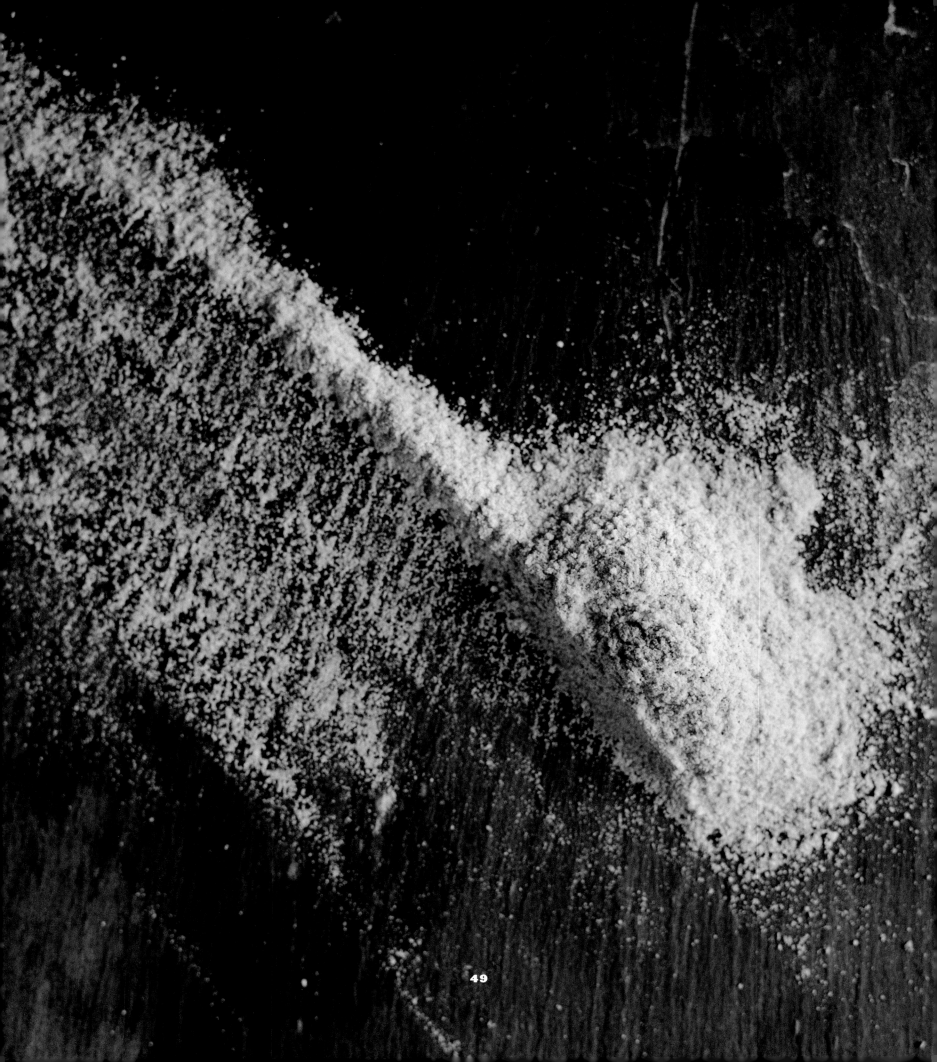

SQUID

*Scientists predict that the biodiversity
of the world's oceans will decrease dramatically
in the future and that squid will therefore become
bigger and stronger.*

69

BIRCH

Freshly cut logs of birch wood.

70

PIKE-PERCH

*Pike-perch can be found in
many of Finland's 187,888 lakes.*

71

FRESH MACKEREL AND GRILLED CUCUMBER

72 (264)

BIRCH WOOD DESSERT

73 (265)

NATIVE OYSTER SHELL

*Native flat oysters have been foraged for centuries,
it is thought that they were an important source of nourishment
to early human hunter-gatherer societies.*

74

SEAWEED

*Seaweed collected from
the Norwegian coastline.*

75

CLAMS

*Fresh clams from the
west coast of Sweden.*

76

FISH TAILS

*Fish tails can form the basis
of a good fish stock.*

77

TURBOT SKIRTS AND CHEEKS, ASPARAGUS AND VERBENA

78 (266)

Søren Brandt Wiuff from Lammefjorden

79 (347)

WINTER CABBAGE AND WINTER OYSTERS

80 (267)

BLUESHELL MUSSELS AND ANGELICA WITH VEAL BREAST

81 (268)

COOKED LEEKS AND CARAMELIZED PORK STOCK, ASHES AND HAZELNUT

82 (269)

TOPAZ APPLE, FRESH HAZELNUTS AND MARJORAM

83 (270)

OYSTERS AND MALT OIL, APPLE AND TAPIOCA

84 (271)

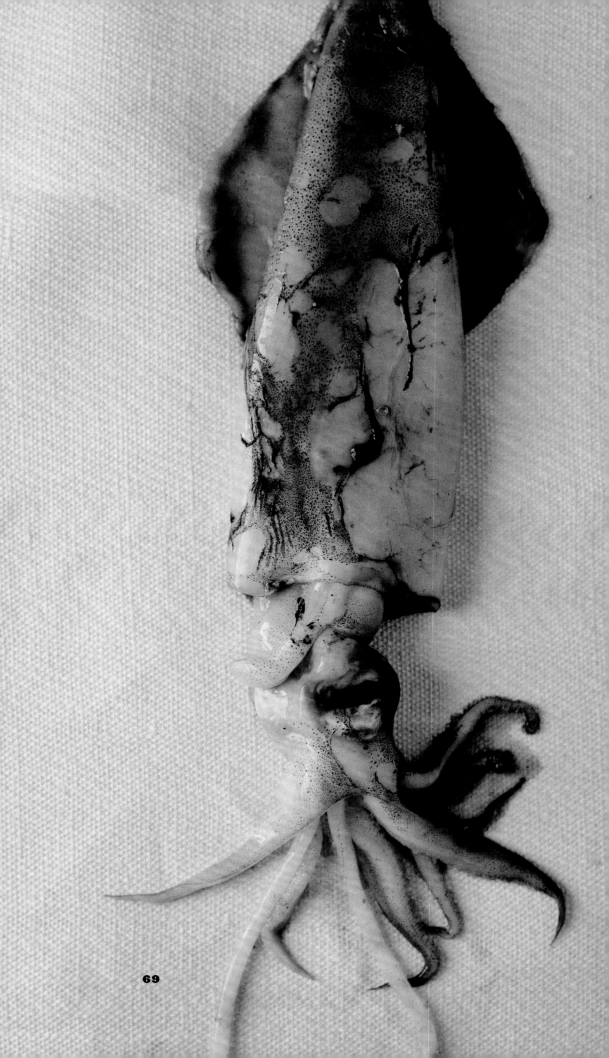

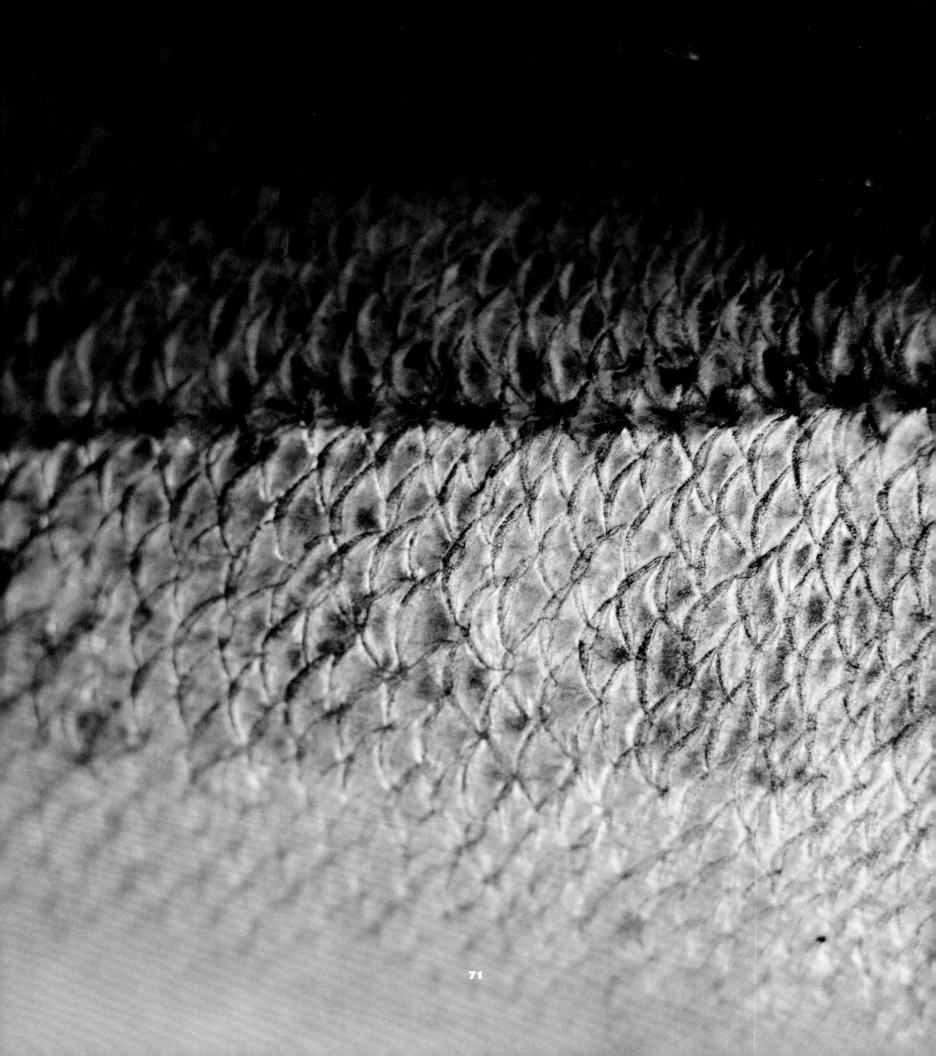

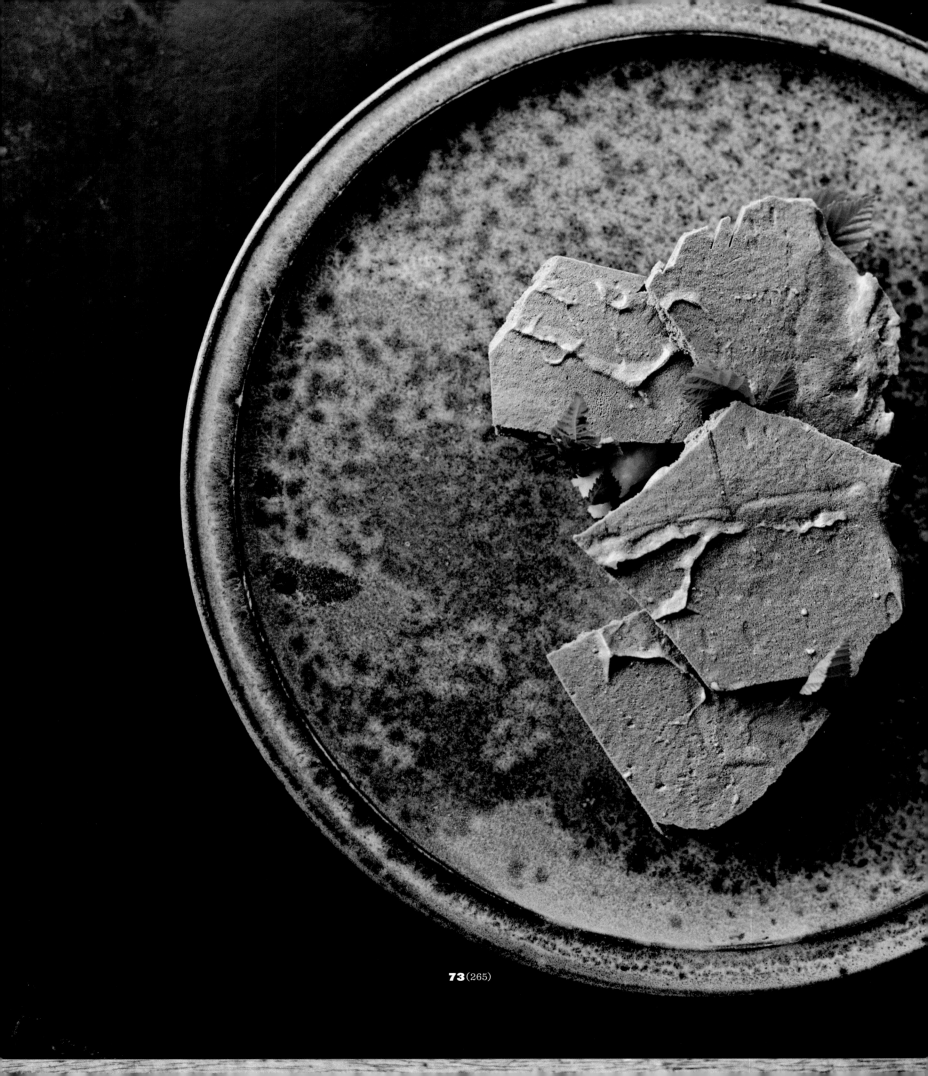

BULRUSHES

Bulrushes have a strong cucumber-like flavour with a light peppery aftertaste.

89

BEANS

The beans at Noma come in many shapes and sizes. They are supplied by Chris Elbo, who grows them organically in his garden on the north coast of Zealand, and tend to peak in quality around the middle of August.

90

Roland Rittman
from
Anderslöv

91 (348)

THUJA CONES

Thuja cones have a powerful flavour and should be used with care.

92

GREEN STRAWBERRIES

Unripe strawberries have an acidic flavour and are crunchier than ripe ones.

93

WILD THYME

The thyme that grows extensively throughout the Nordic region has a more lemony flavour than that grown in the Mediterranean.

94

HORSERADISH

Fresh horseradish is one of the cornerstones of Nordic cuisine, along with vinegar and ryebread.

95

MUSK OX
AND
FRESH YOUNG GARLIC, MILK SKIN
AND
CARAMELIZED GARLIC

96 (272)

BROAD BEANS

Broad beans have been grown in Denmark since the fourteenth century.

97

ROMAINE LETTUCE

The root of the Romaine lettuce is extremely juicy and has a strong nutty flavour when cooked.

98

RAMSONS LEAVES

Commonly known as wild garlic, ramsons grow in most of Copenhagen's parks.

99

GRAPES

In 2006 we planted our own vineyard on the island of Lilleø, using mainly Riesling, Sauvignon Blanc, Sylvaner and Solaris grapes. The first vintage was named after René's daughter, Arwen.

100

FIDDLEHEAD FERNS

Our fiddlehead ferns are sourced from the south of Sweden.

101

DUCK BREAST, TONGUE
AND
HEART, NASTURTIUMS
AND
WATERCRESS

102 (273)

YELLOW STAR
OF
BETHLEHEM

The appearance of the Yellow Star of Bethlehem flower is one of the first edible signs that spring has arrived.

103

TURBOT
WITH
EARLY SPRING HERBS

104 (274)

CAULIFLOWER FLOWERS

The flowers of the cauliflower plant have a delicious, almond-like flavour.

105

POTATOES

Freshly dug 'egg yolk' potatoes.

106

POACHED EGGS
AND
RADISHES

107 (275)

SWEETBREADS
AND
SEAWEED, BLEAK ROE
AND
SEASHORE HERBS

108 (276)

ZEALAND WOODS

These woods overlook Chris Elbo's smallholding in Zealand, north of Copenhagen.

109

BABY CORN

The baby corn supplied by Søren Wiuff has a sweet, liquorice-like flavour.

110

DOVER SOLE
AND
GREEN STRAWBERRIES, BEACH CABBAGE
AND
NEW POTATOES

111(277)

APPLES

Apples grown in Lammefjorden.

112

NORDIC FLORA

Spruce shoots, wood sorrel in flower, woodruff and young beech leaves.

113

FRESH SHRIMP
AND
PICKLED SEAWEED, STONECROP
AND
RHUBARB JUICE

114(278)

CHESTNUTS

Chestnuts do not grow extensively in the Nordic region. Those used at Noma are supplied from private gardens.

115

BABY CUCUMBERS

Baby cucumbers have a similar texture to courgettes.

116

TARTARE
OF
BEEF
AND
WOOD SORREL, TARRAGON
AND
JUNIPER

117(279)

PEAS

Peas start to come into season at the end of the asparagus season.

118

SPINACH STEAMED
IN
TEA

119(280)

VEGETABLE FIELD

120(281)

SWEETBREADS
AND
VEGETABLE STEMS, PARSLEY
AND
SEAWEED
121(282)

BREAST
OF
LAMB
AND
MUSTARD OIL
AND
SØREN'S MANY SALADS
122(283)

VEGETABLES
FROM
LAMMEFJORDEN, SEA BUCKTHORN
AND
GOOSEBERRIES
123(284)

SEA LETTUCE
Sea lettuce has a mild flavour, reminiscent of the ocean.
It is a great alternative to lettuce.
124

DANISH SQUID, GREEN STRAWBERRIES
AND
VERBENA OIL
125(285)

YOGHURT
AND
WHEY, PEAS
AND
CELERY
126(286)

POACHED DUCK EGG
AND
OYSTERS, RAW
AND
COOKED VEGETABLES
127(287)

BEACH CABBAGE
Cabbages grow on the sandy
beaches of western Zealand,
and can be harvested in late spring.
128

ELDERBERRIES

*Elderberries should always
be cooked before being eaten.*

130

BLUE
LOBSTER

*Danish blue lobster, caught
around the island of Læsø.*

131

NORWEGIAN
FJORD

*A beautiful fjord in Arctic Norway,
shot from the window of a small fishing boat.*

132

Roderick
Sloan
from
Bodø

133 (349)

LOBSTER
AND
SALAD LEAVES,
RED CURRANT WINE
AND
ROSES

134 (288)

BLUEBERRIES

*Blueberries grow wild
all over the Nordic region.*

135

BLUEBERRIES
SURROUNDED BY THEIR
NATURAL ENVIRONMENT

136 (289)

BLUE
MUSSELS

*A single blue mussel can lay between
5 and 12 million eggs in one season.*

137

NORWEGIAN
FJORD

*The coastline of a small
fjord in Arctic Norway.*

138

BERRIES

*There are fifty-nine types of edible berry
growing wild across the Nordic region.*

140

WALNUTS

*Every year we buy the full harvest from Chris Elbo's
two walnut trees for use at Noma.*

196

BULRUSHES

*The first young bulrush shoots generally appear
at the end of April or the beginning of May.*

197

SNAILS

*The snails used at Noma are gathered
in the wild by Roland Rittmann.*

198

HAY

*We use hay to smoke food and
the ash of burnt hay as an ingredient.*

199

SEA URCHINS

*Many of the sea urchins at Noma are caught
in ice-cold Arctic waters, but they can be found
in all oceans. The season starts in November
and finishes at the end of February.*

200

BEECH NUTS

*When peeled and roasted, the taste of beech nuts
is somewhere between pine nuts and hazelnuts.*

201

SNAILS
AND
MOSS

202 (321)

POTATO
CRISPS
WITH
ANISE
AND
CHOCOLATE

203 (322)

CHESTNUTS
AND
WALNUTS,
RYE
AND
CRESS

204 (323)

SMOKED
BONE MARROW
AND
ONION,
THYME FLOWERS
AND
VEAL BREAST

205 (324)

RAZOR CLAMS

We first started using razor clams
at Noma in December, 2007.

217

BREAD, BUTTER
AND
FAT

218 (331)

SEA URCHINS
AND
FROZEN MILK, CUCUMBER
AND
DILL

219 (332)

CHICKEN SKIN
AND
RYEBREAD, SMOKED CHEESE
AND
LUMPFISH ROE

220 (333)

SMOKED QUAIL EGGS

221 (334)

GRÅPÆREN PEARS

These Danish pears are similar to Grise-bonne
and are extremely flavourful, with coarse,
juicy flesh. Susanne Grefberg provides
6–8 boxes for Noma every year.

222

STEAMED EGG WHITE
AND
BIRCH WINE, WILD MUSHROOMS

223 (335)

OXTAIL
AND
DARK BEER, APPLE
AND
JERUSALEM ARTICHOKE

224 (336)

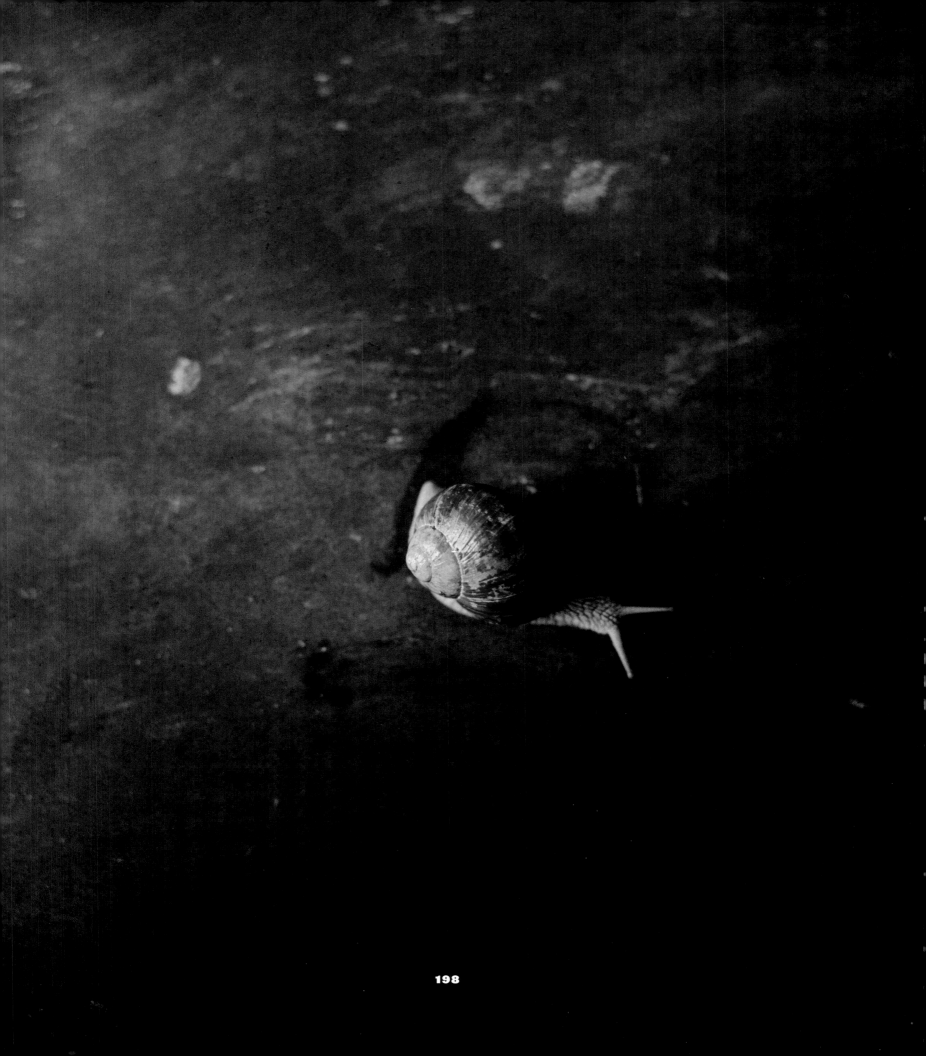

199

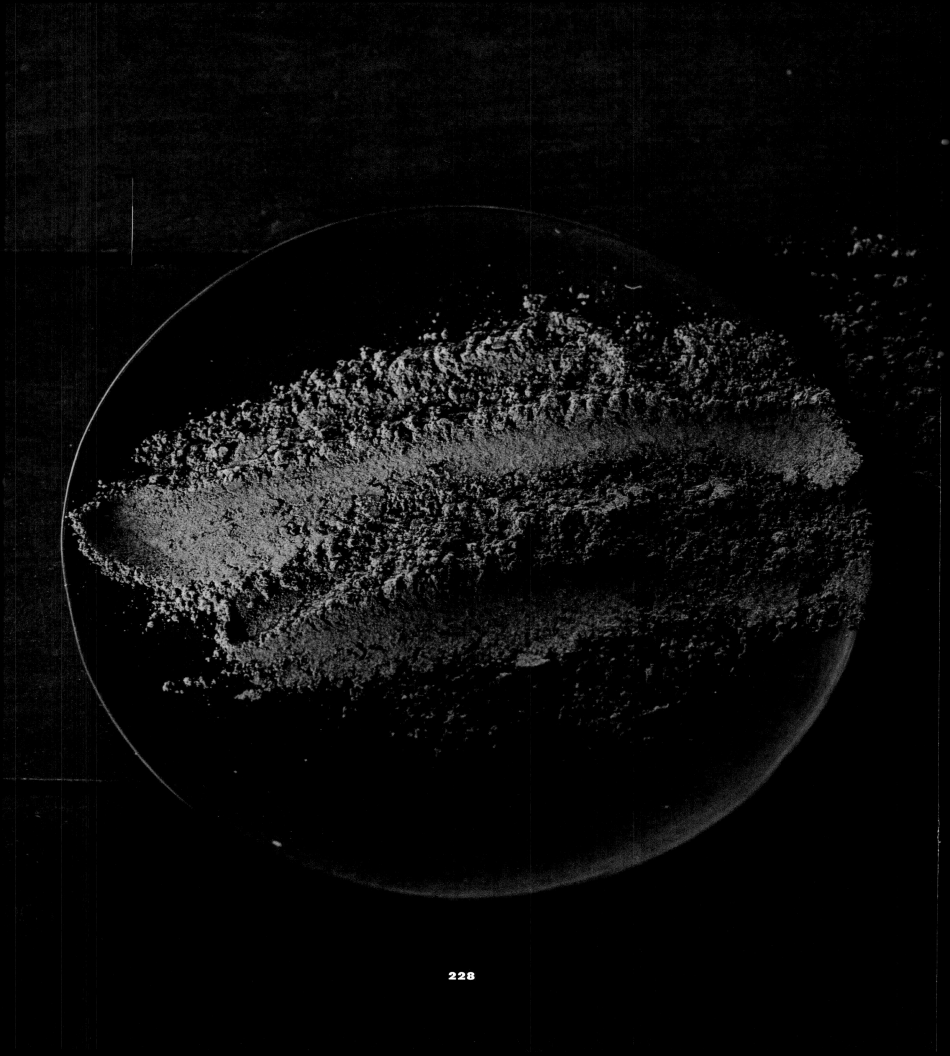

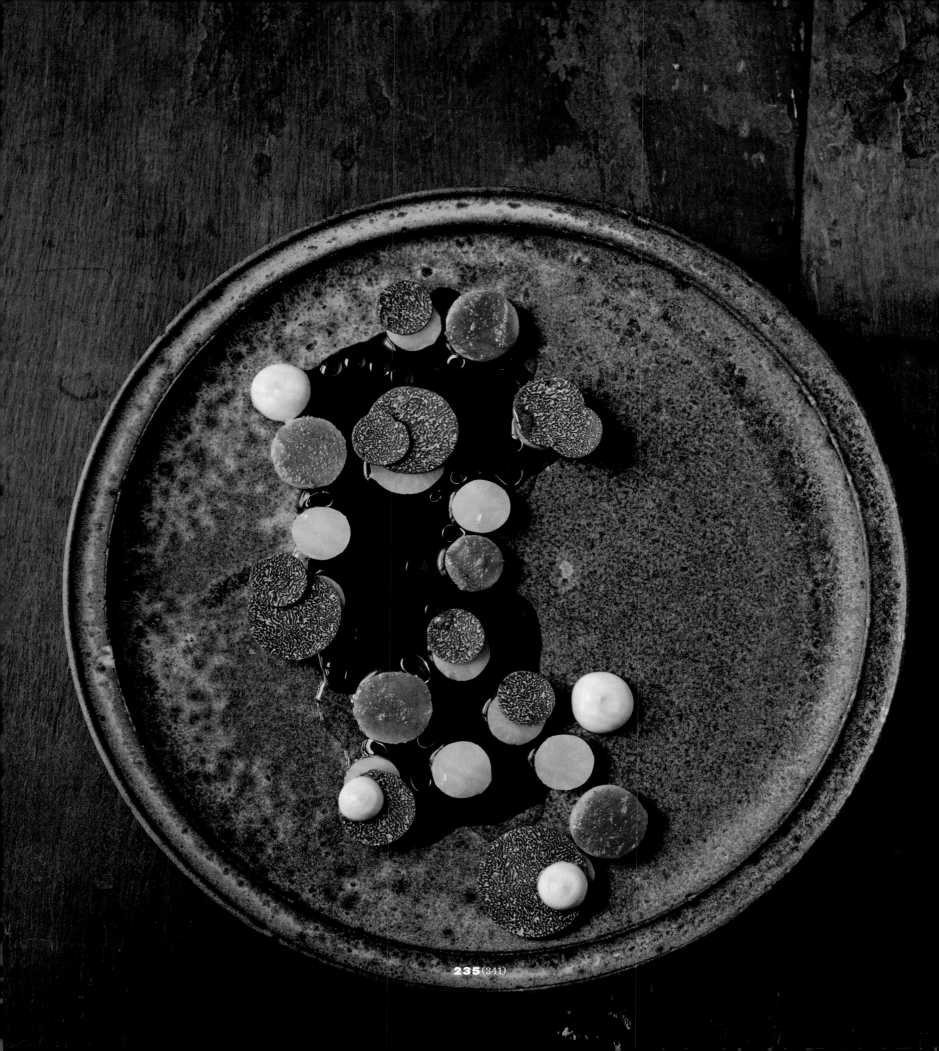

237

WOOD

The restaurant's wooden rafters are
original, and date back to 1766.

244

Réne Redzepi

245

OAK CHAIRS

The chairs at Noma are a Danish design
from 1962. They are all made from oak
which has been smoked for 7 hours.

246

SHEEPSKIN

Diners at Noma sit on Nordic animal
skins, such as this Icelandic sheepskin.

247

RESTAURANT INTERIOR

Noma is on the Copenhagen waterfront and
natural light floods in throughout the day.
Stone, wood and iron are the dominant materials.

248

THE
WEATHER
RECIPES

René Redzepi

CUCUMBER
AND
VERBENA

5 cucumbers
13g verbena leaves
20g lemon juice
70g stock syrup (50% sugar, 50% water)
1g salt
3 leaves gelatine
6g maltodextrin
2g xanthan gum

1 cucumber
40g egg whites
20g sugar
3 leaves gelatine
200g sheep's yoghurt
8g lemon juice
80g double (heavy) or whipping cream

15g egg white powder
130g water
10g apple balsamic vinegar
50g sugar
50g isomalt
7.5g dried verbena

1 cucumber
verbena leaves

Photograph page 46

Cucumber sorbet

Halve the cucumbers and remove the seeds. Cut the cucumber flesh into small pieces, add the fresh verbena leaves and process in a Thermomix for 10 seconds. Leave to macerate for 5 minutes, then strain through a fine cloth. Weigh out 550g of the strained juice (reserve the rest) and add the lemon juice, stock syrup and salt. Bloom the gelatine. Warm a little of the weighed juice mixture and melt the gelatine in it. Whisk in the maltodextrin and then the xanthan gum. Stir into the bulk of the weighed juice mixture and freeze in Paco containers.

Mousse

Slice the cucumber thinly, cutting out the seedy part but keeping the skin. Vacuum-pack in bags with the remaining cucumber juice from the sorbet recipe for 5 minutes. Strain off the liquid and reserve, and pat the slices dry with kitchen paper (paper towel). Cut a sheet of acetate into pieces approximately 8×4cm. Lay cucumber slices on each piece and roll to form a hollow cylinder. Tape the acetate together to keep it tight. Keep the cylinders upright to make it easier to fill them with mousse later. Whip the egg whites and sugar to stiff peaks and place in the refrigerator. Bloom the gelatine. Heat one-fifth of the yoghurt and add the gelatine. Mix with the remaining yoghurt and stir in the lemon juice. Whip the cream and fold it into the yoghurt mixture, then fold the egg white mixture into the yoghurt mixture. Spoon into a piping (pastry) bag and fill the cucumber cylinders. Leave to set in the refrigerator.

Meringue

Dissolve the egg white powder in 100g of the water. Combine the remaining 30g water, the vinegar, sugar and isomalt and heat in a pan to 121°C (250°F). While this caramel is heating whisk the egg white mixture to soft peaks. When the caramel is cooked, whisk it into the egg whites. Add the verbena and keep whisking until the contents of the bowl are cool. Preheat the oven to 55°C (130°F). Spread the meringue on a tray and dry in the oven for 12 hours. When dry, break into small, irregularly sized pieces.

Garnish

Peel the cucumber, cut out small balls of flesh with a parisienne cutter, and vacuum-pack them for 4 minutes in the reserved cucumber juice from the sorbet recipe. Pick out 4–5 shoots of fresh verbena per person and rinse in ice water. Strain the cucumber balls and keep on kitchen paper in the refrigerator.

Serving

Release the mousse-filled cucumber cylinders from the acetate and place one on each plate. Process the sorbet in a Pacojet, shape into a quenelle with a spoon and position one on each plate. Add a few cucumber balls and the verbena shoots, and cover with the meringue pieces.

CEPS
AND
POACHED TRUFFLE MERINGUE

100g **egg whites**
15g **egg white powder**
1g **salt**
2g **apple balsamic vinegar**
80g **truffle from Gotland**

200g **cep (fresh porcini) trimmings**
115g **grapeseed oil**

2 **eggs each weighing approximately** 55–65g
35g **cep (fresh porcini) oil**

1 **loaf white bread**
60g **clarified butter**
salt
80g **ceps (fresh porcini)**

Photograph page 47

Truffle meringue
Whisk the egg whites and the powder into a meringue, adding the salt and vinegar. Chop the truffle finely and fold it through the meringue. Make irregular quenelles on a silpat and steam at 75°C (170°F) for 6 minutes.

Cep oil
Preheat the oven to 80°C (180°F). Place the ceps in a metal container and pour the oil over them. Cover the container tightly with clingfilm (plastic wrap) and cook it in the oven for 12 hours. Strain through a cloth, pour into a small squeezy bottle and keep refrigerated.

Egg yolk vinaigrette
Poach the eggs for 35 minutes at 65°C (150°F), then cool. Remove the yolks, strain and add the cep oil to make a vinaigrette.

Garnish
Freeze the bread and cut into 4 thin slices while still frozen. Preheat the oven to 160°C (325°F). Fold the frozen bread slices into irregular shapes on silpats and spray with the butter. Sprinkle with salt and bake for 7–8 minutes. Clean the ceps with a damp cloth and slice very finely on a mandolin just before serving.

Serving
Place a single meringue in the middle of a plate and dress with the egg yolk vinaigrette. Add the crispy toast and the finely sliced mushrooms.

PORK BELLY
AND
PORK SCRATCHINGS
RAMSONS LEAVES,
SHOOTS,
STEMS
AND
FLOWERS

800g **pork belly (side)**
125g **salt**

200g **pork rind**
1 **onion**
milk, for blanching
1 **potato**
50g **plain (all-purpose) flour**
grapeseed oil, for frying

200g **ramsons (wild garlic) leaves**
425g **light chicken stock**
40g **butter**
30g **chicken glace**
15g **rapeseed (canola) oil**

4 **baby cucumbers**

8 small **ramsons (wild garlic) leaves**
8 small shoots **ramsons (wild garlic)**
24 **ramsons (wild garlic) flowers**

Photograph page 50

Pork belly
Remove the bones and the skin from the meat and sprinkle it with the salt. Let it cure for 24 hours. Rinse the salt from meat and poach it in a vacuum bag at 75°C (170°F) for 12 hours. Cool immediately, and cut into portions when cold.

Pork scratchings
Mince the pork rind straight from the refrigerator, add the minced fat to a pan or pot and start melting slowly at low heat. Keep turning up the heat gradually, stirring from time to time, until the temperature reaches 130°C (265°F). By this time the solid components of the fat should be crisp. Strain off the scratchings and discard the fat. Chop the onions and blanch them in milk for 1 minute. Strain and cool. Dust them with the flour and fry in grapeseed oil at 180°C (350°F) until crisp and golden. Slice the potatoes, fry them in the same oil until crisp, then cool and crush into smaller pieces. Mix together the onions, potatoes and scratchings in equal quantities.

Ramsons sauce
Blanch the leaves in the chicken stock, and cool. Process in a Thermomix for 2 minutes, then strain.

Grilled cucumber
Char-grill (charbroil) the cucumbers on one side only to avoid overcooking them.

Garnish
Pick the leaves, shoots and flowers into ice water and spin them dry. Store on dry paper until you serve the dish.

Serving
Heat the ramsons sauce, add the softened butter and emulsify. Split it with the rapeseed oil. Sauté the portions of pork belly on both sides and sprinkle the crispy scratchings mixture on top. Place on the plate together with the cucumber and the sauce. Arrange the garnish around the meat and serve.

FRESH CHEESE AND SPRUCE SHOOTS

500g **fresh organic full fat (whole) milk**
25g **cream**
10g **buttermilk**
2g **rennet**

200g **sorrel leaves**
100g **spruce shoots**
130g **apple juice**

50g **bread**
butter, for sautéing
spruce shoots
stonecrop berries

Photograph page 51

Fresh cheese
Heat the milk in a pan to 23°C (73°F) and add the remaining ingredients. Pour into covered ovenproof plastic containers and cook in the oven at 36°C (97°F) for 1 hour 25 minutes, or until set with the same consistency as fresh tofu. Cool with the lids off.

Spruce juice
Press the sorrel through a juicer to obtain 100g of juice. Process the juice, spruce shoots and apple juice in a Thermomix for 1 minute at full speed. Pass through a fine-mesh sieve (strainer).

Garnish
Break up the bread into small crumbs, sauté in a warm pan with a little butter, then cool. Pick the herbs, put into ice water and dry.

Serving
Scoop out a small piece of fresh cheese and drain it on a piece of kitchen paper (paper towels). Transfer the cheese to a plate and cover with the spruce shoots, toasted crumbs and stonecrop berries. Pour the juice around the cheese.

ROWAN SHOOTS
AND
MEAD,
FRESH CHEESE
AND
CROUTONS

500g **fresh organic full fat (whole) milk**
25g **cream**
10g **buttermilk**
2g **renne**

125g **acidic and not too sweet mead**
7g **honey**
85g **unsalted butter**

32 **rowan shoots**
2 **slices light white bread**

salt
30g **cold-pressed rapeseed (canola) oil**

Photograph page 52

Fresh cheese
Heat the milk in a pan to 23°C (73°F) and add the remaining ingredients. Pour into covered ovenproof plastic containers and cook in the oven at 36°C (97°F) for 1 hour 25 minutes, or until set with the same consistency as fresh tofu. Cool with the lids off.

Mead sauce
Warm the mead with the honey in a pan and whisk in the butter. Froth with a stick blender until a velvety texture is achieved.

Garnish
Pick the shoots, put into ice water and spin them dry. Keep them cool on kitchen paper (paper towels) until serving. Break the bread up into 10–15 small irregular pieces and toast them in a pan with a little oil for 2–3 minutes until golden and crisp.

Serving
Scoop out a small piece of cheese, drain on kitchen paper and sprinkle with salt. Transfer the cheese to a plate and cover it with the rowan shoots and toasted pieces of bread. Warm the sauce slightly, split it with the rapeseed oil and add to the plate.

MILK ICE
AND
BARLEY,
POACHED EGG
AND
LIQUORICE

300g **milk**
17g **sugar**
40g **trimoline**
50g **cream**
12g **instant food thickener**

150g **pearl barley from Skærtoftmølle**
550g **water**

500g **water**
65g **sugar**
5g **green anise**
8g **liquorice stalks cut in pieces**
12g **instant food thickener**
4g **reduced apple balsamic vinegar**

4 **organic eggs, approximately** 55–65g

Photograph page 54

Milk ice

Heat the milk, and dissolve the sugar and trimoline in a small amount of it. Cool, then add the remaining ingredients, mix thoroughly and freeze in Paco containers. Process immediately before serving.

Barley

Preheat the oven to 160°C (325°F) and toast the barley for 35 minutes. Place in a pan with the water and cook on the stove top until all the moisture has evaporated. Rinse briefly to cool, then put on a cloth to dry in the refrigerator.

Liquorice syrup

Bring the water, sugar, anise and liquorice to the boil, turn off the heat and infuse for 1 hour. Strain the liquid and reduce to half. Thicken with the instant food thickener and season with the vinegar.

Poached eggs

Poach the eggs in a water bath at 65°C (150°F) for 35 minutes.

Serving

Put the plates in the freezer until very cold. Warm the eggs in a water bath at 58°C (135°F) for 20 minutes. Heat the liquorice syrup. Mix the ice cream and the barley, and smear 2 tablespoons of the mixture on the sides of a frozen plate. Crack the eggs open, remove and discard the white, put a yolk on each plate and pour the warm syrup on top.

SNOWMAN

70g **sea buckthorn juice**
50g **sugar**
17g **water**
1.5g **citric acid**
4g **apple balsamic vinegar**
35g **egg whites**
1.5g **egg white powder**
50g **maltodextrine**

375g **carrots**
1.125kg **carrot juice**
4g **sorbet stabilizer**
1.5g **maltodextrine**
312g **stock syrup (50% water, 50% sugar)**
52g **lemon juice**
22g **egg whites**
3 **sheets gelatine**

250g **buttermilk**
250g **yoghurt**
3 **sheets gelatine**

60g **sugar**
25g **water**
5g **apple vinegar**
50g **egg whites**
25g **egg white powder**
8g **white wine vinegar**
50g **maltodextrine**

200g **carrots**
35g **carrot juice**
lemon juice
icing (confectioners') sugar
25g **carrot, brunoised**

350g **water**
75g **sugar**
375g **sheep's yoghurt**
225g **cow's yoghurt**
10g **lemon juice**

4 **baby carrots**

Photograph page 55

Sea buckthorn mousse

Heat the sea buckthorn juice until it has reduced to 50g of liquid and let cool. Combine the sugar, water, citric acid and vinegar in a pan and heat to 121°C (250°F) to make a caramel. Whisk up the egg whites and egg white powder and add the caramel to make an Italian meringue. Fold the sea buckthorn reduction into the meringue and place in the refrigerator. Scoop out small balls into the maltodextrine powder and roll them into round shapes.

Carrot sorbet

Peel the carrots, slice thinly and boil them in 625g of the juice until very tender and all the juice has evaporated. Process in a Thermomix and strain through a cloth. Weigh out 375g of the purée. Heat the stabilizer and the maltodextrine in a little of the stock syrup and mix with the remaining ingredients. Using a refractometer make sure the sugar content of the base is 18°, adding extra water or stock syrup if necessary. Freeze in Paco containers and spin.

Yoghurt glace

Combine the buttermilk and yoghurt and heat in a water bath. Bloom the gelatine and add it to a small amount of the mixture. Scoop out round balls of the carrot sorbet and freeze them in a blast freezer. Skewer the balls with a wooden cocktail stick (toothpick) and line them up on a polysterene plate. Submerge all the balls in liquid nitrogen for 10 seconds and load a spray painting gun with the yoghurt glace. Spray paint the carrot sorbet balls and freeze them. Transfer them to the refrigerator 8 minutes before serving.

Meringue base

Heat the sugar, water and vinegar in a pan to 121°C (250°F) to make a caramel. Whisk the egg whites and egg white powder and add the caramel to make an Italian meringue. Pipe the meringue mixture in 3cm diameter balls into the maltodextrine powder and dehydrate at 72°C (162°F) for 10 hours.

Carrot purée

Peel the carrots, cut into thin slices and vacuum-pack them. Cook the bag in boiling water until the carrots are tender, then purée them with the juice in a blender. Season with lemon juice and icing sugar, and fold in the carrot brunoise.

Yoghurt snow

Mix all the ingredients and freeze in Paco containers. Scrape the mixture to obtain a snow-like texture, and freeze again.

Serving

Chill the plates. Place a spoonful of carrot purée in the middle of each plate. To build the snowman first add the meringue base, then place the glazed carrot sorbet on top. Place a ball of sea buckthorn mousse on top of the sorbet and add the point of a baby carrot to simulate the nose. Sprinkle yoghurt snow around the plate.

CARAMEL
AND
MALT

65g **sugar**
200g **cream**
65g **milk**
80g **egg yolks**

83g **sugar**
185g **cream**
50g **milk**
9g **milk powder**
70g **egg yolks**
12.5g **trimoline**
½ **sheet gelatine**

125g **sugar**
250g **cream**
250g **milk**
7g **milk powder**
90g **egg yolks**
65g **trimoline**
2 **leaves gelatine**

Day 1
175g **flour**
85g **malt powder**
50g **hazelnut flour**
25g **sugar**
75g **beer**

Day 2
40g **flour**
20g **malt powder**
50g **hazelnut flour**
4g **fine salt**
60g **melted butter**

100g **sugar**
1g **malt flour**

30g **skyr**

Photograph page 58

Caramel cream
Heat 45g of the sugar in a pan until it begins to caramelize, then deglaze completely with the cream and milk. Heat to 80°C (180°F). Whisk the remaining 20g sugar with the egg yolks in a bowl and pour the warm liquid over this mixture. Preheat the oven to 150°C (300°F). Hand blend the caramel mixture and cook in a gastro in a bain-marie in the oven for 70 minutes. Cool, stir and put in a piping (pastry) bag.

Caramel ice cream
Heat 45g of the sugar in a pan until it begins to caramelize, then deglaze completely with the cream and milk, and add the milk powder. Heat to 80°C (180°F). Whisk the remaining 38g sugar with the egg yolks in a bowl and pour the warm liquid over this mixture. Cook as though making a custard. Bloom the gelatine and add to the mix before it cools. Process in an ice cream machine.

Caramel siphon
Heat the sugar in a pan until it begins to caramelize, then deglaze completey with the cream and milk, and add the milk powder. Heat to 85°C (185°F) and pour some of the mixture over the egg yolks and trimoline while whisking. Pour back into the rest of the mixture and cook as for a custard. Bloom the gelatine and add to the mixture before it cools. When cool, pour into a siphon bottle and add 1 cartridge.

Malt soil
Day 1
Preheat the oven to 90°C (195°F). Mix all the dry ingredients in a bowl and pour into a food processor. Process 3 times in short bursts while adding the beer. Spread out on a tray and dry in the oven for 3–6 hours. When dry, sift out the thickest lumps.

Day 2
Follow the mixing procedure from *Day 1*, starting with the dry ingredients and then adding the butter. Combine the 2 batches throughly by hand. Make sure no moist lumps are left in the mixture.

Malt tuile
Preheat the oven to 160°C (325°F) and grease a baking tray. Heat the sugar to 155°C (310°F) to make a dry caramel and cool on a silpat. Process in a Thermomix to a fine powder and sift on to the trays. Bake for 2–3 minutes, cool, and when cold break into smaller pieces.

Serving
Put some bowls into the freezer to get very cold. Process the ice cream and load it into a piping bag. Pipe or siphon the caramel cream, ice cream and siphon into a frozen bowl, then add the skyr. Sprinkle the malt soil on top and add the pieces of malt tuile.

BOUILLON
OF
STEAMED BIRCHWOOD, CHANTERELLES
AND
FRESH HAZELNUT

200g **small or medium chanterelle mushrooms**
20g **butter**
a little bouillon
salt

1 litre **light chicken stock**
400g **piece of birch**
2.5g **thuja cones**
1g **dried woodruff**
2.5g **dried verbena**
1g **black tea leaves**
4 **egg whites**
reduced white wine
apple balsamic vinegar

300g **fresh hazelnuts**
2–3 **small fresh ceps (porcini)**

Photograph page 59

Chanterelles

Clean the bottoms of the chantarelles by scraping them with a small knife. Dip them very briefly in water to rinse off any dirt – don't let them stay in the water too long or they will absorb too much. Heat the butter in a pan until foamy and toss the chantarelles in it for a few seconds so that they are warmed through but maintain their structure. Add a few tablespoons of the bouillon to glaze. Season with salt and let the chantarelles drain on kitchen paper (paper towels) before serving.

Bouillon

Preheat the oven to 90°C (195°F). Put the stock and birch wood in a deep gastro and cover it with clingfilm (plastic wrap). Cook in the oven for 12 hours. Add the cones, dried herbs and tea and let them infuse in the warm bouillon for 5 minutes. Strain, reduce to one-third and let cool. Lightly whisk the egg whites, add to the bouillon and heat slowly to clarify. Pass the bouillon through a cloth and season to taste with wine and vinegar.

Hazelnuts and ceps

Crack the hazelnuts and scrape off the fine brown skin. Slice them finely on a mandolin just before serving. Scrape the bottoms of the ceps and wipe the upper part with a damp cloth. Make sure there is no dirt left on them, then slice them as finely as the hazelnuts.

Serving

Heat the bouillon and place all the chanterelles in a deep bowl. Cover them with the sliced hazelnuts and ceps and pour the bouillon on top.

ASPARAGUS, BULRUSH AND DUCK EGGS

4 **duck eggs**

4 **bulrushes**
8 **stems white asparagus**
40g **water**
100g **butter**

125ml **red currant wine**
85g **unsalted butter**
5g **woodruff leaves**
50g **spinach leaves**

16 **beech shoots**
12 **hop shoots**
2 **ciabatta-style loaves**
butter, melted
salt

Photograph page 62

Poached duck eggs
Poach the eggs at 65°C (150°F) in a water bath for 36 minutes and cool in ice water.

Bulrush and asparagus
Trim the bulrushes down to the tender middle part at the bottom. Peel the white asparagus and cut the tips at an angle approximately 3cm down the stem. From the middle section of the remaining asparagus, cut 5 round pieces of asparagus per person. Each piece being approximately 1cm long. Heat the water and whisk in all the butter to emulsify it.

Woodruff sauce
Heat the red currant wine and add the butter in small dice while blending with an immersion blender. Wash and dry the woodruff and spinach. When cool, process the sauce with the leaves in a Thermomix.

Garnish
Rinse the beech and hop shoots in water and keep them dry on kitchen paper (paper towels) until serving. Freeze the bread for a few hours. When still half frozen split lengthways, then slice to obtain small round toasts of approximately 2cm diameter. Preheat the oven to 160°C (325°F). Spread out the toasts on baking trays, brush with plenty of melted butter and sprinkle with salt. Bake in the oven for 6 minutes. Turn the trays and bake for another 6 minutes. Ensure the toasts are kept warm before serving.

Serving
Cook the asparagus tips in the butter emulsion for 35 seconds, then add the rounds and cook for another 15 seconds. Strain off the butter and season the asparagus with salt. Cook the bulrushes in the same way for 15 seconds and season with salt. Heat the eggs to 58°C (135°F) and crack them open to pull out the yolks. Place a yolk in the centre of each plate and arrange bulrushes and asparagus around it. Heat the sauce without allowing it to boil, and add it to the plate together with the toasts and shoots.

AEBLESKIVER
AND
VINEGAR
MERINGUES

15g **sugar**
32g **water**
15g **apple balsamic vinegar**
50g **egg whites**

85g **egg yolks**
125g **cream**
125g **tipo '00' flour**
65g **butter, melted**
1g **ground cardamom**
2.5g **salt**
150g **egg whites**

40g **maltodextrin**
12g **freeze dried white wine vinegar powder**
7g **salt**

Photograph page 63

Vinegar meringues
Combine the sugar, vinegar and water in a large pan and heat to 121°C (250°F). Whisk the egg whites to soft peaks, take the pan off the heat and pour the syrup slowly into the mixture, still whisking, to make an Italian meringue. Keep whisking the mixture until the bowl has cooled. Using a piping (pastry) bag, pipe small round meringues of approximately 25 mm diameter. Dry in a dehydrator at 55°C (130°F) for 12 hours.

Batter
Whisk together the egg yolks, cream and finally the flour. Cool the melted butter to room temperature and add to the mixture with the cardamom and salt. Whisk the egg whites until stiff and fold into the batter. Cook in an aebleskiver pan, and when half cooked add the small meringues. Keep turning and filling the aebleskiver until it is completely round and the batter is cooked through, making sure that the meringue stays crisp within the fluffy casing.

Vinegar powder
Mix together the maltodextrin, vinegar powder and salt.

Serving
When the aebleskiver is cooked, roll it in the vinegar powder while still warm. Dust off the excess powder and serve.

Aebleskiver are a traditional Danish sweet, cooked from a dough similar to that used in French pancakes and shaped into small balls in a special aebleskive pan. They have been recognized as a Danish delicacy since the seventeenth century.

WHITE CURRANTS AND GELLED CUCUMBER JUICE, SWEET CICELY AND HAZELNUT MILK

2 **cucumbers, picked freshly**
salt
lemon juice, to season
6 **leaves gelatine**

300g **blanched and peeled hazelnuts**
300g **water**
salt

8–10 **white currant twigs**
12 **shoots sweet cicely**

cold-pressed rapeseed (canola) oil

Photograph page 64

Cucumber gel
Juice the cucumbers, pass the juice through a sieve (strainer) and season with salt and the lemon juice. Measure out 300ml of the juice and bloom the gelatine. Warm up a small amount of the liquid and melt the gelatine in it. Mix with the rest of the juice and pour into round, domed moulds of approximately 4cm diameter.

Hazelnut milk
Process the hazelnuts and water for 1 minute in a Thermomix and leave to macerate for 24 hours. Strain, and push through a Superbag to obtain a silky hazelnut milk. Season to taste with salt.

Berries and garnish
Break up the whitecurrant twigs into smaller pieces and rinse them in water. Pick the sweet cicely into ice water and spin the shoots dry. Store on kitchen paper (paper towels) until serving.

Serving
Put the plates in the refrigerator to get cold. Remove the gel from the moulds and ensure it has reached room temperature before serving. Place each piece of cucumber gel on a cold plate and arrange the berries and garnish around the gel. Split the hazelnut milk with rapeseed oil and serve.

POTATO CRISPS AND YOGHURT

4 small Ratte potatoes
oil, for frying
salt

125g **buttermilk**
125g **yoghurt**
3g **gelatine**

Photograph page 65

Potato crisps (chips)
Slice the potatoes with a Japanese turning vegetable slicer and fry them in oil. Drain on grease absorbent paper and season with salt. Drop them into liquid nitrogen until frozen solid.

Yoghurt glace
Mix the buttermilk and yoghurt and heat in a water bath at 50°C (120°F). Bloom the gelatine and add it to a little of the yoghurt mixture, continue heating the mixture until the gelatine has melted. Load a spray gun and spray the crisps with the yoghurt glazing while they are still frozen. Keep the crisps in the freezer until 5 minutes before serving.

CLOUDBERRIES
FROM
PITEÅ,
BURNT MERINGUE
AND
HERBAL TEA

100g **water**
2g **sorbet stabilizer**
42g **glucose**
56g **sugar**
500g **cloudberry purée**
juice of 1 orange

3.5g **pectin**
30g **cane sugar**
1 kg **water**
8g **dried blueberry leaves**
5g **dried blackcurrant leaves**
1.2g **dried mint**
1.2g **dried yarrow**
2g **dried woodruff**
4.5g **Earl Grey tea leaves**

145g **sugar**
65g **water**
100g **egg whites**
12g **apple balsamic vinegar**

Photograph page 66

Cloudberry sorbet
Heat the water with the stabilizer, glucose and sugar. When cool, mix with the purée and juice. Freeze in Paco containers.

Herbal tea granita
Mix the pectin in a little of the sugar and bring it to the boil with some of the water. Heat the rest of the water and pour it over the herbs, leaves and the remaining sugar. After 4 minutes strain and cool, and combine with the pectin and sugar mixture. When completely cold, freeze in a flat container. Scrape the granita to a powder with a fork once frozen.

Burnt meringue
Heat the sugar and water to 121°C (250°F) to make a caramel. Whisk the egg whites to soft peaks and add the caramel slowly, still whisking, to make an Italian meringue. Add the vinegar, and keep in a piping (pastry) bag.

Serving
Put the plates into the refrigerator to get cold. Process the sorbet in a Pacojet and load it into a piping bag with a 1.5-cm nozzle (tip). Pipe out into long tubes and cut these to 2cm lengths. Store the sorbet pieces in the freezer. Pipe meringue in small dots on to a cold plate and burn the tops with a blowtorch. Arrange 7–8 pieces of sorbet on the plate, scatter the granita on top and serve.

FRESH MACKEREL
AND
GRILLED CUCUMBER

2 small, extremely fresh mackerel

2 large cucumbers
500g water
30g apple balsamic vinegar
50g sprigs dill
4 baby cucumbers

15g cornflour (cornstarch)
90g milk
500g buttermilk
75g horseradish, grated
lemon juice
salt

24 nasturtium leaves

20g dill oil

Photograph page 72

Mackerel
Skin and bone the mackerel and divide each fillet in to 2 to give 4 long pieces in all.

Cucumber
Peel the large cucumbers, cut into slices about 8mm thick and trim them into perfect rounds. Blend the water, vinegar and dill sprigs, then strain. Pickle the cucumbers in a vacuum bag with the liquid for 10 minutes. Reserve the liquid to serve later. Grill the baby cucumbers on a barbecue on one side only.

Horseradish snow
Mix the cornflour and milk, boil, stirring, until thick and smooth, then cool for 10 minutes. Mix with the buttermilk and horseradish and leave to infuse for 12 hours. Strain off the horseradish and season to taste with lemon juice and salt. Freeze in Paco containers. When frozen, spin for 10–15 seconds in the Pacojet. A snow-like texture will be created on the surface of the horseradish mixture. Scrape it off and repeat the procedure until you have enough for 8–10 tablespoons. Keep in the freezer.

Garnish
Pick the leaves, keeping as long a stem as possible on each. Rinse in ice water and dry on kitchen paper (paper towels).

Serving
Place each mackerel fillet on a cold plate and arrange cucumber slices around the plate. Add a grilled baby cucumber and some nasturtium leaves to each plate. Split a few tablespoons of the reserved pickling liquid with the dill oil, add some horseradish snow to the plate and pour some sauce around the fish. Finally, sprinkle salt on the fish and snow.

BIRCH WOOD DESSERT

50g **isomalt**
50g **sugar**
50g **water**
100g **birch water**
10g **egg white powder**
40g **birch syrup**

200g **planed birch wood**
500g **birch water**

2 **sheets gelatine**
500g **birch stock**
30g **glucose**
2.5g **maltodextrin**
40g **sugar**
15g **lemon juice**

1 ½ **sheets gelatine**
20g **honey**
200g **acidic mead**
1.5g **fresh verbena**

12 **tips of wild chervil leaves**

Photograph page 73

Meringues

Mix the isomalt, sugar and water in a large pan and heat it to 121°C (250°F) to make a caramel. Mix the birch water and egg white powder and whisk until light and airy. Add to the caramel when it is cooked, continuing to whisk. Add the birch syrup and keep whisking until the meringue has cooled. Preheat the oven to 60°C (140°F). Spread the meringue mixture on baking trays and dry in the oven for 12 hours.

Birch stock

Bring the wood and water to the boil and leave it to rest for 6 hours. Strain the liquid and reduce it to half.

Birch sorbet

Bloom the gelatine. Mix the stock, glucose, maltodextrie and sugar in a large pan, bring to the boil. Add the gelatine and lemon juice and freeze in Paco containers.

Mead gel

Bloom the gelatine. Bring the honey and mead to the boil in a pan. Mix in the verbena and gelatine and let it infuse for 30 minutes. Strain off the verbena, pour the rest into a bowl and place in the refrigerator to set.

Wild chervil

Pick the leaves and let them soak in ice water for a few minutes. Spin them dry and keep cool until serving.

Serving

Put the plates in the freezer to get very cold. Break up the gel into small, irregular pieces and put 3 tablespoons on to a frozen plate. Process the sorbet in the Pacojet and add 3 tablespoons to the plate. Break up the meringues and arrange them on top of the gel and sobet, finally add the chervil between the pieces of meringue.

TURBOT SKIRTS
AND
CHEEKS,
ASPARAGUS
AND
VERBENA

skirts and cheeks from 1 turbot
45g **salt**
125g **water**
200g **butter, cubed**

50g **spinach**
5g **verbena leaves**
125ml **red currant wine**
15g **honey**
85g **unsalted butter, cubed**
spinach

4 **thick stems white asparagus**

butter emulsion
small verbena leaves

Photograph page 78

Turbot
Sprinkle the turbot with the salt and leave to cure for 24 hours. Heat the water in a pan and emulsify the butter in it. Bring the emulsion to the boil, remove the pan from the heat and add the turbot. Leave for 3–4 minutes, then pull off the small, meaty pieces of fish and discard the skin and bones.

Verbena sauce
Wash and dry the spinach and verbena. Heat the red currant wine and honey in a pan and add the butter while blending with a hand blender. When the sauce is cool, process it in a Thermomix with the spinach and verbena. Keep on ice until serving to preserve colour and flavour.

Asparagus
Peel the asparagus and cut off the tops 10cm down the stem. Thinly slice the tops and soak them in plenty of ice water for 10 minutes. Strain, and dry on kitchen paper (paper towels). Cut the middle part of the rest of the asparagus stems into rounds and discard the bottoms. Blanch the rounds for 1 minute.

Serving
Warm 4 bowls. Heat the verbena sauce slightly and add the cooked fish. Warm the asparagus rounds in the butter emulsion. Pour the sauce into a warm bowl and arrange the asparagus rounds and raw asparagus around it. Garnish with the small verbena leaves.

WINTER CABBAGE
AND
WINTER OYSTERS

12 medium Danish oysters from Limfjorden

100g **water**
250g **butter**
5g **hay, finely chopped**

1 **white cabbage**

1 **green cabbage**
1 **black cabbage**
1 **savoy cabbage**
1 **pointed cabbage**

4 **big leaves savoy cabbage**
½ **clove garlic**
1 **shallot**
8 **sprigs thyme**
350g **white cabbage**

105g **baby spinach**
10g **verbena leaves**
250g **red currant wine**
85g **unsalted butter**

Photograph page 80

Oysters
Shuck the oysters carefully with an oyster knife and remove them from their shells. Strain the natural liquid and rinse the oysters in it. Strain the liquid again and heat slightly. Poach the oysters in the liquid for a few seconds to firm them up.

Smoked butter emulsion
Heat the water in a medium pan, cut the butter into pieces and whisk it in to emulsify. Burn the hay with a smoke gun, or hand-held food smoker, fill the pan with smoke and cover with a lid. Let it infuse for a few minutes until the smoke has disappeared. Repeat a few times untill a smoky aroma emanates from the emulsion.

White cabbage disc
Preheat the oven to 100°C (200°F). Cut the cabbage into very fine slices, retaining the basic shape. Stack 4 slices on top of each other with small sheets of baking (parchment) paper in between, and brush all the slices with the smoked butter emulsion. Vacuum-pack the bags in a single stack and steam them in the oven for 10 minutes.

Different types of cabbage
For each person, trim a single leaf of green cabbage, leaving a small piece of stem on the leaf. Trim a black cabbage stem, leaving a few tender leaves at the top. Punch out a big leaf of savoy cabbage to approximately 4cm diameter. Trim a single piece of pointed cabbage per person down to the stem, and peel off the tough outer layer. Rinse all the cabbage pieces and keep cool until serving.

Cabbage roll
Blanch the savoy cabbage leaves in salted water and cool them in ice water. Place on kitchen paper (paper towels) to dry. Chop the garlic, shallot and thyme and sauté in a little oil. Slice the white cabbage finely and add to the sauté pan, letting it cook slowly until caramelized. Cool the cabbage mixture in a sieve (strainer) to release all the liquid and add a tablespoon of the smoked emulsion. Spread out the savoy cabbage leaves and make sure they are completely dry. Add a few tablespoons of the compote, roll up the cabbage and trim the sides.

Verbena sauce
Wash the spinach and verbena and place on kitchen paper to dry. Heat the red currant wine in a pan, dice the butter and add it to the wine, blending with a stick blender. When cool, process the sauce in a Thermomix with the spinach and verbena.

Serving
Warm the smoked butter emulsion and drop the different types of cabbage into it. Heat the white cabbage discs on a hot surface and place on the plate. Make sure the stems of the various cabbage types have cooked tender but that the leaves have remained crisp, then arrange them on the plate together with the oysters. Add the cabbage roll. Warm the verbena sauce very slightly and add.

BLUESHELL MUSSELS

AND

ANGELICA

WITH

VEAL

BREAST

200g **veal breast**
oil, for frying

1kg **mussels**
a little vinegar
18g **angelica leaves**
150g **grapeseed oil, plus extra for sautéing**
lemon juice
salt

Photograph page 81

Fibres

Vacuum-pack the veal breast and cook in a water bath at 80°C (190°F) for 10 hours, then pull it apart into its natural fibres. It is easiest to do this if the meat is kept warm. Fry the meat in oil at 160°C (325°F) and drain on kitchen paper.

Mussel emulsion

Wash the sand from the mussels and soak them for about an hour in water containing a little vinegar. Blanch in salted water for 10 seconds and remove from the shells. This quantity of mussels in the shell should give approximately 100g of meat. Sauté the meat briefly in a little oil in a very hot pan, and cool. Chop the angelica roughly (reserve a few small leaves for garnish) and mix with the mussels in a Thermomix bowl. Process, and add the oil in a thin stream while blending as if making a mayonnaise. Season with lemon juice and strain. Pour into a piping (pastry) bag and keep very cold.

Serving

Roll the fibres into a small ball for each person and insert the nozzle (tip) of the piping bag into the centre. Fill up with the mussel emulsion, then scatter the reserved small angelica leaves on the ball. Sprinkle with salt and serve.

COOKED LEEKS
AND
CARAMELIZED
PORK STOCK,
ASHES
AND
HAZELNUT

10 **big leeks**

green tops from the leeks
45g **dill oil**

125g **hazelnuts**

140g **yoghurt**
20g **red currant wine**

2.5kg **pork ribs cut in small pieces**
1 **onion**
½ **apple**
2 **sticks celery**
5 **sprigs thyme**

Photograph page 82

Leeks
Cut the green tops off the leeks, and reserve. Blanch the lower white part for 9 minutes in salted water. When cool remove the outer layers and keep only the inner 1cm. Cut each leek in half lengthways.

Ash purée
Wash and dry the leek tops and grill them on a barbecue until completely dried and burnt. Sieve the ashes, weigh out 45g and mix with the oil.

Hazelnut purée
Preheat the oven to 160°C (325°F). Toast the nuts in the oven for 20 minutes. While still warm, blend them to a fine purée.

Yoghurt sauce
Mix a little of the yoghurt with the red currant wine, then fold this mixture into the rest of the yoghurt.

Caramelized pork stock
Preheat the oven to 230°C (450°F). Roast the ribs for 30 minutes until golden brown. Peel the onion and apple and pan-roast them. Reduce the oven temperature to 80°C (180°F). Combine everything in a deep gastro tray and add water to cover. Cover the gastro with a lid and cook in the oven for 10 hours. Strain the liquid and reduce to a glace-like consistency. Preheat the oven to 70°C (160°F). Spread the mixture on silpats and dry in the oven for 10 hours. Keep in an airtight container until serving.

Serving
Cover the cut side of 3 of the half leeks with the ash purée and 2 with the hazelnut purée. Arrange them lengthways across a large plate and add the yoghurt sauce to the middle of the plate. Crumble a tablespoonful of the caramelized stock over the dish.

TOPAZ APPLE,
FRESH
HAZELNUTS
AND
MARJORAM

4 **Topaz apples**
icing (confectioners') sugar
gelatine, in 2-g **leaves**

300g **blanched and peeled hazelnuts**
300g **water**

6 **Topaz apples**
sea salt
10g **grapeseed oil**
5g **fresh marjoram leaves**
apple balsamic vinegar

apple balsamic vinegar, aged for 9 years

Photograph page 83

Apple gel and powder
Peel the apples and dry the peel for 24 hours in a dry place. Blend to a fine powder. Cut the apples and put them through a vegetable juicer. Pass the juice through a very fine cloth. Measure the sugar content with a refractometer, and add icing sugar until it reaches 15°. Weigh the juice and calculate 1 leaf of gelatine per 100g of juice. Bloom the gelatine, then melt it in a small amount of the juice. Set in the refrigerator.

Hazelnut milk
Process the hazelnuts and water for 1 minute in a Thermomix and macerate for 24 hours. Strain and push the mixture through a Superbag.

Apple compote
Preheat the oven to 90°C (195°F). Peel 4 of the apples and rub with salt, oil and marjoram leaves. Place in a roasting tray, cover and cook in the oven for 1 hour. Scrape the cooked apple flesh from the core with a spoon, without stirring too much. Season with salt and add extra apple balsamic vinegar to increase the acidity if necessary. This compote should be made shortly before serving and kept at room temperature as it will lose flavour if left to cool.

Serving
Peel the remaining 2 apples and slice thinly on a mandolin, then cut into rounds of approximately 2cm diameter. Break up the apple gel and place a spoonful in the centre of a deep bowl together with the compote. Sprinkle the apple powder on top and build several slices of apple around the central components. Drizzle a tablespoon of hazelnut milk around the apples and a few drops of aged vinegar over the dish.

OYSTERS
AND
MALT OIL,
APPLE
AND
TAPIOCA

250g **water**
15g **apple balsamic vinegar**
25g **dill stems**
4 **Topaz apples**

40g **powdered malt**
100g **grapeseed oil**

100g **tapioca pearls**
1 litre **water**
50g **cream**
20g **full fat (whole) milk**

4 big Danish oysters from Limfjorden

Photograph page 84

Pickled apples
Mix the water, vinegar and dill stems to make a brine. Process in a Thermomix for 2 minutes and strain. Peel the apples and slice them thinly on a mandolin. Cut the slices into 2cm diameter circles with a cutter and vacuum-pack the slices with the pickling brine for 10 minutes.

Malt oil
Mix the malt and oil and process in a Thermomix for 3–4 minutes. Keep in a squeezy bottle.

Tapioca cream
Wash the tapioca in running water, then put in a large pan with the measured water. Bring to the boil and cook for about 10 minutes then rinse the tapioca in cold water to cool it. Mix the cream and milk and add enough tapioca to give a stew-like consistency.

Oysters
Carefully open the oysters with an oyster knife and release them from their shells. Blanch for 10 seconds in water to firm them up. Immediately before serving, cut the oyster into 3 equally sized slices.

Serving
Put 3 pieces of oysters on each plate and arrange the apple slices around them. Pour the tapioca cream around and on the oysters, shake the squeezy bottle containing the malt oil and drip a little over the cream.

MUSK OX
AND
FRESH YOUNG GARLIC, MILK SKIN
AND
CARAMELIZED GARLIC

400g **musk ox loin**
grapeseed oil, for sautéing
45g **chicken glace**

1kg **full-fat milk**
50g **cream**
30g **milk protein**
4 **new season garlic bulbs**
salt

90g **chicken glace**
apple balsamic vinegar

24 **leaves onion cress**

12 **small shoots garlic**
grapeseed oil, for brushing on

20g **brown butter**
5g **finely chopped shallots**
2g **finely chopped parsley**
5g **ramsons (wild garlic) capers**

Photograph page 96

Musk ox
Cut the meat into four 100-g portions. Roll tightly in clingfilm (plastic wrap) and poach at 58°C (135°F) for 10–12 minutes. Wipe the meat dry and sauté it in the oil in a very hot pan. Add the chicken glace to glaze.

Milk skin
Preheat the oven to 200°C (400°F). Mix the milk, cream and milk protein together in a pan and heat everything to around 70°C (160°F). Skim off the first few skins, which will be very fragile. When a firm skin has formed, pull it off with both hands and store it on baking (parchment) paper. Repeat until 8–10 perfect skins have been produced. Bake the garlic in the oven for 20 minutes, squeeze out the soft interior and season the resulting purée with salt.

Sauce
Warm up the chicken glace and season with the vinegar.

Garnish
Pick the leaves of the onion cress into ice water, spin them dry and keep cool on kitchen paper (paper towels) until serving.

Burned young garlic
Just before serving, brush the garlic with the oil and char-grill (charbroil) until soft in the middle and burnt on the outside.

Serving
Heat the milk skins on a hot surface or by putting them in a hot oven for 2 minutes, smear the garlic purée over them and then roll them up into a cigar shape. Put 2 on each plate and arrange the burnt garlic around them. Place the meat next to them and the herbs around each plate. Add the brown butter, shallots, parsley and capers to the sauce. Pour onto the plate and serve.

DUCK BREAST, TONGUE
AND
HEART,
NASTURTIUMS
AND
WATERCRESS

1 duck breast
35g clarified butter
500g water
35g salt
4 duck tongues
125g light duck stock
2 sprigs thyme

140g picked watercress
20g water
30g apple balsamic vinegar
6g Dijon mustard
220g grapeseed oil

5 bunches thyme (to make 42g when blanched)
small bunch parsley (to make 12g when blanched)
55g grapeseed oil

2 very ripe sweet Gråpære pears
4 small leeks
salt

32 nasturtium leaves

butter, for sautéing
2 duck hearts
35g duck glace
15g brown butter
5g chopped shallots
5g ramsons (wild garlic) capers

Photograph page 102

Duck
Score the fat on the duck breast, brush the fat-free side with the clarified butter, and leave uncovered in the refrigerator for 6–7 days. Combine the water and salt to make a brine and vacuum-pack the tongues in it for 24 hours. Rinse off the salt, vacuum-pack the tongues with the duck stock and thyme, and steam the bag at 80°C (180°F) for 12 hours. Remove the cartilage from the tongues while still warm and let them cool in the stock.

Watercress emulsion
Process the watercress, water, vinegar and mustard in a Thermomix, and while mixing pour in the grapeseed oil as quickly as possible. Strain through a fine cloth and keep on ice until serving. Add extra vinegar to increase the acidity if necessary.

Thyme oil
Blanch the thyme on its stems for 4–5 minutes until very tender. Cool in ice water and pull off the stems. Strain to obtain all the leaves and squeeze through a Superbag to remove the remaining water. Keep dry on kitchen paper (paper towels). Pick the leaves from the parsley stalks and blanch them tender. Dry as for the thyme. Process the oil and herbs in a Thermomix at full speed at 60°C (140°F) for 12 minutes. Cool, then macerate for 24 hours. Strain through a fine cloth, applying pressure for a few hours, and keep in a small squeezy bottle.

Pears and leeks
Peel the pears and cut them lengthways in thick slices. Remove the cores and char-grill (charbroil) 1 slice of pear per person on 1 side. Take the pears off the heat and rub thyme oil and salt into them to taste. Blanch the leeks in salted water for 2 minutes and cool in ice water. Char-grill the leeks on 1 side only and finish as for the pears.

Garnish
Pick the leaves, put into ice water and spin them dry in a salad spinner. Keep them dry and cool until serving.

Serving
Place the duck breast skin-side down in a cold sauté pan and bring it slowly to low heat. Leave the meat to cook until the fat is very crisp and add a piece of butter. Baste the breast a few times with the butter, turn to cook the other side for a few seconds, then rest for 8 minutes before carving. Sauté the duck hearts in butter for a few seconds and add the duck glace. Heat the tongues in a tablespoon of brown butter together with the shallots and capers. Place the pears and leeks on the plates, carve the breast into 4 pieces, divide each heart into 2 and distribute all the meat among the plates. Warm the sauce without boiling, then add to the plates and finish with nasturtium leaves.

TURBOT
WITH
EARLY SPRING HERBS

1 large organic celeriac (celery root), peeled
1kg **water**
1kg **plain (all-purpose) flour**
600g **salt**

1kg **peeled and diced celeriac (celery root)**
grapeseed oil, for sautéing
40g **brown butter**
240g **cream**
60g **water**
salt

140g **watercress leaves**
20g **water**
30g **apple balsamic vinegar**
6g **Dijon mustard**
220g **grapeseed oil**

100g **butter**
20g **water**
8 **large ramsons (wild garlic) leaves with stems**
20 **small shoots ramsons (wild garlic)**
4 **shoots and flowers of cowslips**

1 **small turbot of around** 1kg
grapeseed oil, for sautéing
butter
thyme

60g **water**
50g **butter**

Photograph page 104

Baked celeriac
Preheat the oven to 220°C (425°F). Mix the water, flour and salt to a dough, roll out and cover the celeriac completely. Bake for 10 minutes, then reduce the oven temperature to 160°C (325°F) and bake for a further 35 minutes. Cool, then cut out long, round sticks with an apple corer.

Celeriac purée
Sauté the celeriac in grapeseed oil on one side until lightly golden, drain off the excess fat, cool and vacuum-pack. Put the vacuum bag in a pan with some boiling water and cook for 35 minutes or until very tender. In the meantime, reduce the cream to one-third. Dice the cooked celeriac, blend with the rest of the ingredients until smooth, season with salt and pass through a fine cloth.

Watercress emulsion
Put the watercress, water, vinegar and mustard in a Thermomix, process, then pour in the oil while continuing to mix as quickly as possible. Strain the mixture through a fine cloth and keep on ice until serving. Add extra vinegar to increase the acidity just before serving if necessary.

Garnish
Cut the stems off the ramsons leaves. Heat the water and whisk in the butter to make an emulsion. Pick the shoots, leaves and flowers from each other, leaving as much stem as possible.

Turbot
Take the flesh off the bone with a sharp pointed knife, cut the skin off and divide the fish into 50-g portions. Sauté on one side in grapeseed oil in a warm pan, finish off with a piece of butter and the thyme, basting it for a few seconds. Be careful not to overcook the fish.

Serving
Heat the water and whisk in the butter to make an emulsion. Drag half a tablespoonful of the celeriac purée across the plate, heat the baked celeriac in the butter emulsion and add the ramsons stems for the last few seconds. Gently warm the watercress emulsion. Plate the turbot along with the celeriac, stems, flowers and shoots, and accompany with the slightly warm watercress sauce.

POACHED EGGS
AND
RADISHES

4 organic eggs, each weighing approximately 55 – 65g

50g **sea lettuce**
45g **vinegar**
90g **water**

3 **long black radishes**
2 **long red radishes**
3 **white radishes**
2 **yellow radishes**

125ml **red currant wine**
15g **honey**
85g **unsalted butter**
5g **verbena leaves**
50g **spinach**

40g **butter**
40g **water**

Photograph page 107

Poached eggs

Poach the eggs in a water bath at 65°C (150°F) for 35 minutes until soft poached.

Pickled sea lettuce

Rinse the sea lettuce very thoroughly to remove any sand. Combine the vinegar and water and leave the sea lettuce in the mixture for 1 hour to pickle it. Spread the pickled sea lettuce out on sheets of baking (parchment) paper, ensuring that the paper is entirely covered. Cut the paper into 13cm diameter rounds with a pair of scissors.

Radishes

Wash and rub the radishes to clean them, then cut in 8-mm slices. Briefly blanch the radish slices in salted water, then cool in ice water.

Verbena sauce

Heat the red currant wine and honey, then add the butter in small dice while blending with a hand blender. Wash and dry the verbena and spinach. Add them to the sauce when it has cooled, and process in a Thermomix.

Serving

Heat the eggs to 58°C (135°F) in a water bath and crack them open to remove the yolks. Place an egg yolk in the middle of each plate. Heat the water, cut the butter into pieces and whisk it into the water to form an emulsion, then heat the radishes in the butter emulsion. Heat the verbena sauce. Place radish rounds all the way around the egg yolk, and drizzle sauce in between everything. Heat the sea lettuce on the baking paper rounds on a hot surface, then cover the entire dish with the sea lettuce.

SWEETBREADS AND SEAWEED, BLEAK ROE AND SEASHORE HERBS

8 **shoots sea purslane**
16 **shoots beach mustard**

300 – 400g **veal sweetbreads**
25g **butter**

200g **fresh dulse (söl)**
50g **sea lettuce**
150g **white wine vinegar**
300g **water**

100g **white wine**
60g **butter**
60g **bleak roe from Kalix in Sweden**

Photograph page 108

Seashore herbs

Pick the leaves into ice water and spin them dry. Keep them cool on dry kitchen paper (paper towels) until serving.

Sweetbreads

Trim any excess fat and sinew from the sweetbreads and cut them into 4 portions. Sauté them dry in a pan at medium heat on their flattest side for 6 – 7 minutes, by this time the surface touching the pan should be very crisp. Add the butter to the pan and when it is foaming baste the upper side of the meat. Turn the sweetbreads and cook them for 30 seconds on the other side. Leave to rest on kitchen paper for 2 minutes before serving.

Seaweed

Rinse all the seaweed very thoroughly to get rid of any sand. Pickle the sea lettuce by rinsing it briefly in a mixture of the vinegar and water. Immediately before serving, heat the water in a pan and plunge the dulse in it for 2 seconds to heat it.

Sauce

Heat the white wine in a pan, reduce to one-third and whisk in the butter while still warm. Add the bleak roe immediately before serving.

Serving

Place the sweetbreads in the middle of the plate and arrange all the warm seaweed around them. Cover the sweetbreads with the bleak roe sauce and arrange the herbs on top of the seaweed

DOVER SOLE
AND
GREEN STRAWBERRIES, BEACH CABBAGE
AND
NEW POTATOES

2 **Dover sole**

8 **green strawberries**
12 **nasturtium leaves**

20 **small new potatoes**
coarse salt, for scrubbing
125g **water**
200g **butter, diced**
2 **stems lovage**
12 **stems beach cabbage**

90g **chicken glace**
apple balsamic vinegar

oil and butter, for sautéing
20g **brown butter**
5g **finely chopped shallots**
2g **finely chopped parsley**
5g **ramsons (wild garlic) capers**

Photograph page 111

Fish

Skin and fillet the soles to give 4 equal portions.

Strawberries and nasturtiums

Remove the tops and slice the strawberries thinly on a mandolin. Keep them stacked together until serving. Pick the nasturtium leaves, put into ice water and spin them dry. Keep cool on kitchen paper (paper towels) until serving.

New potatoes and beach cabbage

Scrub the potatoes with coarse salt to remove impurities from the skin. Heat the water, whisk in the butter to emulsify and add the lovage. Just before serving, cook the potatoes in this butter emulsion until *al dente*. Rinse the cabbage pieces and add them to the warm emulsion with the potatoes for the last 1 minute of cooking.

Sauce

Heat the chicken glace and add extra vinegar to increase the acidity if necessary.

Serving

Sauté the fish in a little oil in a very hot pan for a few minutes on the inner side of the fillets. Add a piece of butter at the end and baste the fish a few times. Drain on kitchen paper and let the fish rest for a minute or so before serving. Place a fillet in the middle of each plate and arrange the potatoes and cabbage around it. Add strawberry slices and nasturtium leaves to the plate. Quickly reheat the sauce and add the brown butter, shallots, parsley and capers at the last minute, then add to the plate.

FRESH SHRIMP AND PICKLED SEAWEED, STONECROP AND RHUBARB JUICE

20 deep water shrimp

500g **sea lettuce**
450g **vinegar**
900g **water**

1 **stick rhubarb**
50g **stock syrup (50% water, 50% sugar)**
grapeseed oil
salt

110g **rhubarb juice**
80g **beetroot (beet) juice**
50g **apple balsamic vinegar**
50g **stock syrup**

16 **small stonecrop leaves**
24 **small sea purslane leaves**
24 **small beach mustard leaves**

Photograph page 114

Raw shrimp
Carefully shell the shrimp, starting at the tail end and working towards the head. Line up the shelled shrimp on a plate and cool on ice.

Sea lettuce
Rinse the sea lettuce very thoroughly to remove any sand. Mix the vinegar and water and and leave the sea lettuce in the mixture for 1 hour to pickle it. Spread the sheets of sea lettuce out on baking (parchment) paper to cover the whole surface in a single layer. Cut the paper into 13cm diameter rounds with a pair of scissors.

Rhubarb slices
Trim and peel the rhubarb and cut into small slices. Vacuum-pack them with the stock syrup for 6 minutes, then strain. Add a little grapeseed oil and season with salt before serving.

Rhubarb juice
Mix the rhubarb and beetroot juices, the vinegar and stock syrup together and strain.

Herbs
Pick the leaves into ice water and spin them dry. Keep in the refrigerator until serving.

Serving
Remove the cold plate of shrimp from the refrigerator as late as possible. Season the shrimp and cover with a sheet of the pickled seaweed. Add the rhubarb slices, the herbs and finally a few tablespoons of the rhubarb juice.

TARTARE
OF
BEEF
AND
WOOD SORREL,
TARRAGON
AND
JUNIPER

250g **beef fillet (tenderloin)**

125g **tarragon** (2–3 bunches)
1 **small shallot**
1 **clove garlic**
35g **apple balsamic vinegar**
50g **chicken glace**
150g **grapeseed oil**
4g **instant food thickener**

8g **juniper berries**
3g **caraway seeds**

1 **small piece horseradish**
1 **small shallot**
40g **wood sorrel**
10g **rye bread, crumbled**
a little butter

salt
mustard oil

Photograph page 117

Tartare
Trim the meat free of sinews and scrape it lengthways with a large, sharp knife. Make sure the meat keeps some texture, and avoid chopping it or scraping it too finely. Arrange the strands of meat to form a small square per portion.

Tarragon emulsion
Pick the tarragon off its stems and rinse the leaves carefully. Peel and chop the shallot and garlic. Mix everything together in a Thermomix bowl, then mix in the vinegar and chicken glace. Process to emulsify with the oil and strain. Add the instant food thickener and place in the refrigerator to set.

Juniper powder
Toast the berries and seeds in a dry pan to release the aromas, then blend them to a coarse powder.

Garnish
Peel the horseradish and scrape it into long fine pieces with a knife. Slice the shallot thinly, to give 2–3 rings per person. Pick the stems from the wood sorrel and soak them in ice water to crisp up. Spin them dry and store in the refrigerator until serving. Fry the rye bread with a piece of butter until golden and crisp.

Serving
Arrange the meat on a plate and season it with salt and mustard oil. Add 6–7 strings of horseradish and the toasted rye bread. Finally cover the meat entirely with wood sorrel leaves. Sprinkle the juniper powder next to the meat and smear a spoonful of the tarragon emulsion on the plate. Serve with a warm, moistened napkin as this dish is to be eaten without cutlery.

SPINACH STEAMED IN TEA

250g **butter**
100g **water**
2.5g **woodruff**
2.5g **verbena**
1g **black tea**

120g **baby spinach leaves**
8g **lovage leaves**
8g **parsley leaves**
salt and pepper

4 **sticks celery**

20 **dill leaves**
20 **goosefoot leaves**
20 **sprigs chervil**
2 **slices light white bread**
salt

125g **1-year-old Västerbotten cheese**
250g **water**
1g **salt**

Photograph page 119

Tea emulsion
Remove the butter from the refrigerator and let it warm to room temperature. Boil the water and whisk in the butter, infuse this mixture with the dried herbs and tea for 4 minutes, then strain.

Spinach and herbs
Rinse the spinach and leaves thoroughly to remove all dirt. Pull off the stems and discard. Steam the herbs for 1 minute in 4 table-spoons of the tea emulsion, then add the spinach and another spoonful of emulsion, steam for a further 20 seconds and season to taste. Spread the mixture on a small sheet of baking (parchment) paper inside round cutters of approximately 80mm diameter.

Celery
Peel the celery and remove any remaining fibrous strings. Cut horizontally into small pieces.

Herbs and bread garnish
Pull the herb leaves from the stalks, drop the leaves into ice water and strain. Keep on dry kitchen paper (paper towels). Pull the bread into small pieces and sauté them in a pan with butter. Remove when crisp and season with salt.

Cheese sauce
Cut the cheese into small pieces and mix with the remaining ingredients in a Thermomix for 5 minutes at 50°C (120°F).

Serving
Cook the celery pieces for 1 minute in the tea emulsion. Gently heat the discs of spinach and herbs, place one on each plate and put the celery, bread pieces and herbs on top. Foam up the warm sauce with an immersion blender and add the foam to the plate.

VEGETABLE FIELD

Vegetables may vary throughout the seasons:
4 **orange carrots**
4 **yellow carrots**
4 **radishes**
4 **black, green and red radishes**
4 **baby leeks**
1 **baby celeriac (celery root)**
1 **Jerusalem artichoke**
4 **baby parsley (Hamburg) roots**
60g **water**
50g **butter**

80g **peeled potatoes**
5g **butter**
15g **cream**
25g **water**

Day 1
175g **flour**
85g **malt flour**
50g **hazelnut flour**
25g **sugar**
75g **lager**

Day 2
40g **flour**
20g **malt flour**
50 **hazelnut flour**
4g **salt**
60g **butter, melted**

2g **freshly pressed horseradish juice**
12 **leaves from carrot tops**
4 **leaves from parsley root tops**

Photograph page 120

Vegetables

Peel the carrots, leaving 1cm of the tops behind (to use later), then cut them in half and keep tops and bottoms separately. Wipe the radishes and leeks free of dirt and cut them in the same way as the carrots. Scrape the celeriac and the artichoke and quarter them. Cut the tops of the parsley roots off, rinse them in water and then halve them. Blanch all the vegetables in salted water until tender. Heat the water and whisk in the butter to make an emulsion.

Purée

Boil the potatoes and crush them with a fork. Add the rest of the ingredients while the potatoes are still warm.

Malt soil

Day 1: preheat the oven to 90°C (195°F). Mix all the dry ingredients in a bowl and pour into a food processor. Process 3 times in short bursts while adding the beer. Spread on a tray and dry in the oven for 3–6 hours. Push through a coarse sieve to remove the thickest lumps.

Day 2: repeat the mixing procedure from Day 1 with the remaining malt soil ingredients, then mix the 2 batches together by hand, ensuring that no moist lumps are left in the mixture.

Serving

Heat the vegetables in the butter emulsion. In a separate pan, heat the purée, seasoning it with a little horseradish juice to taste. Place a small spoonful on a stone and arrange the vegetables to make them look as though they are sticking up from the ground. Sprinkle the malt soil on top. Pick and rinse the leaves and sprinkle them on top of everything.

SWEETBREADS
AND
VEGETABLE
STEMS,
PARSLEY
AND
SEAWEED

300g **veal sweetbreads**
20g **salt**
5 **juniper berries**
1 **sprig thyme**
2 **bay leaves**
120g **duck fat**

400g **parsley**
salt

1 **cauliflower**
1 **stick celery**
1 **bunch watercress**
4 **stems leek (the stem is obtained when the leek has been
left to flower before harvesting)**
4 **stems carrot (obtained in the same way as the leek stem)**
65g **sea lettuce**
45g **dulse (söl)**
50g **white wine vinegar**
100g **water**

125ml **red currant wine**
15g **honey**
85g **unsalted butter**

15g **chicken glace**
a little butter
salt and pepper

Photograph page 121

Sweetbreads
Remove all the sinews from the sweetbreads, sprinkle the salt and flavourings over them and then leave to cure for 24 hours in the refrigerator. Scrape off the flavourings, vacuum-pack with the duck fat and steam for 9 minutes at 100°C (210°F). Cool in ice water then cut into portions of 50g per person.

Parsley purée
Wash the parsley, pick the leaves from the stems and blanch the leaves for 2–3 minutes until tender. Squeeze out all the water and freeze the parsley leaves in Paco containers. To make a purée spin it in the Pacojet twice, pass through a cloth and season with salt.

Vegetable stems and seaweed
Break the stems of the cauliflower off and peel away the woody outer layer. Repeat the procedure with the celery and cut it to around 9cm in length. Remove the leaves from the watercress and keep them for another dish. Peel the leek and carrot stems, pulling off the outer layer with the tip of a knife. Blanch the cauliflower and celery stems for 3 minutes and the leek and carrot stems for 1 minute. Rinse the salt from the 2 seaweeds, then wash the sea lettuce in the water and vinegar to quickly pickle them.

Red currant sauce
Warm up the red currant wine with the honey and whisk in the butter, then froth with a stick blender until the sauce has a velvety texture.

Serving
Sauté the sweetbreads in a pan on their flattest side for 4–5 minutes or until crisp. Add a spoonful of chicken glace and glaze them in the pan. Heat the vegetable stems in a few tablespoons of butter, adding the watercress stems at the last moment. Warm the parsley purée and pour a quantity of it into the centre of the plate. Drain the stems, season and arrange around the purée. Add the seaweed, the sweetbreads and finally the sauce.

BREAST OF LAMB
AND
MUSTARD OIL
AND
SØREN'S
MANY SALADS

140g **salt**
2 kg **water**
1 **small breast of lamb** (approximately 1.5kg)

2 **romaine lettuces with roots**
4 **mustard leaves**
8 **rocket (arugula) leaves**
8 **watercress leaves**
4 large **Treviso radicchio leaves**
1 **cauliflower**

225g **romaine lettuce leaves**
1 **egg**
9g **chicken glace**
¼ **clove garlic**
50g **grapeseed oil**
4g **instant food thickener**

90g **reduced lamb glace**
apple balsamic vinegar

45g **chicken glace**
butter, for sautéing
salt
20g **cold-pressed rapeseed (canola) oil**
5g **ramsons (wild garlic) capers**
5g **finely chopped shallots**
2g **finely chopped parsley**

Photograph page 122

Breast of lamb

Mix the salt and water to make a brine. Carefully bone the lamb breast, losing as little meat as possible. Vacuum-pack the meat with the brine for 24 hours. Rinse the salt from the meat and vacuum-pack it. Cook in a water bath at 63°C (145°F) for 24 hours, and cool. When cold, cut out 2 small squares of 35–40g per person.

Salads

Remove the outer leaves from the romaine lettuces and discard. Cut out the roots with a knife. Remove the tough outer skin of the roots and halve them. Blanch the roots for 2 minutes in salted water, then cool in ice water. Soak all the leaves in ice-cold water and rinse any dirt from them. Cut the stems off the cauliflower and use the florets for another dish. Peel the stems and remove the fibrous strings on the outside. Blanch the stems for 1–2 minutes depending on size.

Salad emulsion

Rinse the romaine lettuce leaves, blanch until tender and cool. Boil the egg for 7 minutes, then break open and remove the soft yolk. Warm the chicken glace a little to soften it. Blend the leaves, yolk, garlic and glace. Emulsify the oil into the mix. Strain, and add the instant food thickener.

Sauce

Warm the lamb glace and season with the vinegar.

Serving

Sauté the lamb on the skin side until crisp, then add the chicken glace to glaze it all over. Sauté the salad roots briefly in a warm pan, and heat the leaves by pouring a few tablespoons of warm butter over them. Warm the stems in a little water and butter. Put the lamb on the plate and add a few smears of the salad emulsion. Strain excess butter from the salad leaves, season with salt and add to the plate. Arrange the stems and leaves around the plate and add the rapeseed (canola) oil, chopped shallots, parsley and capers seconds before serving.

VEGETABLES
FROM
LAMMEFJORDEN,
SEA BUCKTHORN
AND
GOOSEBERRIES

500g **fresh organic full fat (whole) milk**
25g **cream**
10g **buttermilk**
2g **rennet**

4 **orange baby carrots**
4 **white carrots**
2 **baby celeriac (celery root)**
4 **baby leeks**
1 **large leaf Swiss chard**
1 **small fennel bulb**
2 **mini pointed cabbages**
80g **water**
125g **butter**

1 **stem goosefoot**
1 **fennel top**
4 **leek flowers**

100g **chicken glace**
35g **brown butter**
5g **shallots**
2g **parsley**
apple balsamic vinegar

28 **sea buckthorn berries**
20 **green gooseberries**

Photograph page 123

Fresh cheese
Heat the milk in a pan to 23°C (73°F) and add the remaining ingredients. Pour into covered ovenproof plastic containers and cook in the oven at 36°C (97°F) for 1 hour 25 minutes, or until set with the same consistency as fresh tofu. Cool with the lids off.

Vegetables
Peel all the vegetables and cut the tops off. Keep a small tip of the greens and halve the vegetables so they can stand on a plate. Blanch all the vegetables in salted water for 1–3 minutes depending on type and size. Heat the water in a pan and whisk in the butter in small pieces to emulsify.

Herbs
Pick the goosefoot and fennel, put into ice water, dry and keep cold. Do not wash the flowers or they will spoil – cut them directly into a container.

Brown butter sauce
Heat the chicken glace and add the brown butter without emulsifying. Chop the shallots and parsley and add to the sauce. Season with vinegar to taste.

Serving
Scoop out a piece of cheese from the container and drain it on kitchen paper (paper towels). Heat the vegetables in the butter emulsion. Place the berries in a sieve (strainer) and drain the vegetables over them so that the berries are warmed. Put the cheese on a plate with the vegetables standing up around it. Sprinkle the goosefoot, fennel and berries on top. Heat the sauce, pour it over the cheese and place the leek flowers on top.

DANISH SQUID, GREEN STRAWBERRIES AND VERBENA OIL

1 Danish squid

240g **fresh verbena**
60g **fresh parsley**
180g **grapeseed oil**
45g **cream**
25g **milk**

175g **green strawberries**
icing (confectioners') sugar

1 **bunch dill**
1 **pot tarragon**
4 **green strawberries**
25g **rye bread, grated**
butter, for frying

salt

Photograph page 125

Squid
Remove the body from the head. Cut the body open and scrape on both sides with a knife to clean it. Freeze the squid, and when frozen cut into portions of 6×3cm. Cut each portion into small dice and combine the dice together to form squares.

Verbena oil and cream
Pick the verbena and parsley leaves off their stems and blanch the leaves tender. Squeeze through a Superbag to remove the remaining water. Keep dry on kitchen paper (paper towels). When fully dry, weigh the herbs and add the equivalent weight of the grapeseed oil. Process at full speed at 60°C (140°F) in a Thermomix for 12 minutes. Cool, then macerate for 24 hours. Strain through a fine cloth, applying pressure for a few hours. Mix the cream and milk and keep in the refrigerator until serving.

Green strawberry granita
The strawberries must still be green, but should be ripe enough to be soft on the inside and produce juice when pressed. Remove the tops and rinse the berries in water. Pass them through a vegetable juicer, and strain the resulting liquid. Measure the sugar content with a refractometer and adjust it to 17° with either water or icing sugar. Pour into a metal container and freeze. When frozen, scrape the granita to a powder with a fork and keep in the freezer until serving.

Herbs and garnish
Pick the herbs, put into ice water and dry them. Cut off the tops and rinse the strawberries in water. Slice them thinly on a mandolin. Fry the rye bread in a pan with butter until golden and crispy.

Serving
Put the plates in the refrigerator to get cold. Place a small square of squid in the centre of each plate. Sprinkle with salt and the rye bread crumble. Add the tarragon and dill and mix the verbena oil with the cream and milk mixture, then add to the plate. Add the green strawberries, then the granita and serve.

YOGHURT
AND
WHEY,
PEAS
AND
CELERY

250g **double (heavy) or whipping cream**
50g **egg yolks**
40g **sugar**
200g **yoghurt**
1g **salt**

125g **stock syrup**
150g **water**
10g **lemon juice**

1 **stick celery**
50g **sweet tender young peas**
50g **mangetouts (snow peas)**
12 **pea shoots**
12–16 **mint leaves**
12–16 **wild chervil leaves**

55g **mint sprigs**
55g **grapeseed oil**

500g **yoghurt**

Photograph page 126

Yoghurt parfait
Whip the cream lightly and keep it cool. Whisk the egg yolks and sugar together until airy. Fold in the yoghurt and salt. Fold the whipped cream into the mixture, pour into freezing trays about 2cm high, and freeze. Once frozen, cut the parfait into 5-cm squares and keep frozen.

Vegetable syrup
Mix the stock syrup, water and lemon juice together and keep cool.

Vegetables
Cut the celery in small pieces and blanch briefly in boiling salted water. Blanch the peas and mangetout in the same way. Pick the herbs and refresh them in ice water. Vacuum-pack all the vegetables with the vegetable syrup for 12 minutes. Dry, and keep cool until serving.

Mint oil
Pick the mint leaves from their stems and blanch until tender. Squeeze the leaves through a Superbag to lose all the water. Leave to dry on kitchen paper (paper towels) for a few hours, then process at full speed with the oil in a Thermomix for 12 minutes at 60°C (140°F). Cool, and macerate for 24 hours. Strain through a fine cloth, applying pressure for a few hours.

Whey
Hang the yoghurt in a cloth over a bowl for 24 hours to release the whey from the solids.

Serving
Put the plates in the freezer to get very cold. Place the yoghurt parfait in the middle of a frozen plate and arrange all the herbs and vegetables on top. Mix the whey with the mint oil and drizzle a few spoonfuls around the parfait.

POACHED DUCK EGG AND OYSTERS, RAW AND COOKED VEGETABLES

4 duck eggs

selection of vegetables in season

4 Danish oysters from Lammefjorden
50g smoked bacon, cut into small pieces
1 small shallot, chopped
lemon juice
5g dill

flakes of salt

Photograph page 127

Duck eggs
Poach the eggs at 65°C (150°F) for 36 minutes and cool in ice water.

Raw and cooked vegetables
This recipe should include as many seasonal vegetables as possible, both cooked and raw. It is important to vary the ways of cutting the cooked vegetables and the size of the pieces, in order to give as complex an experience as possible. However, as a general rule we try to keep the vegetables as natural as possible, ensuring each piece is cut small enough to fit into one mouthful, but not so small that it loses its identity. The actual choice of vegetables depends on what is best on the day, and must be judged on the day by the cook. The raw vegetables should be cut into fine, crunchy, thin pieces.

Oyster sauce
This sauce must be made just before serving. Open the oysters and cut each into 5–6 pieces, reserving the liquid. Sauté the bacon lightly in a pan, add the shallots and continue cooking until soft. Add half the oyster juice to the pan, and finally the oyster pieces. Season with a few drops of lemon juice, and make sure the oysters are only slightly warm. Chop the dill and add it to the sauce. Put the remaining oyster juice in a humidifier to spray the egg with when serving.

Serving
Warm the egg, remove the yolk from the white and add the yolk to the centre of a plate. Spray it with the oyster juice, discarding the egg white. Arrange all the vegetables around the yolk, sprinkle everything with flakes of salt and pour the oyster sauce on to the yolk.

LOBSTER
AND
SALAD LEAVES, RED CURRANT WINE
AND
ROSES

2 whole, live lobsters, approximately 600g each
125g **water**
100g **butter**

95g **cream**
80g **lobster stock**
25g **fresh egg yolk**
20g **lobster coral**
6g **instant food thickener**

2 **romaine lettuces with roots**

125ml **red currant wine**
15g **honey**
85g **unsalted butter, cubed**

16 *Rugosa* **rose petals pickled in apple balsamic vinegar**

butter, for sautéing and for an emulsion
oil, for sautéing
sprig thyme

Photograph page 134

Lobster
Push the tip of a strong, sharp knife through the centre of the cross on the lobster's head, cutting all the way through to the chopping board. Remove the head and tail from the body and break off both claws. Remove the knuckles from the claws and reserve for the sauce. Remove any coral from the tail, blanch it for 30 seconds, then cool in ice water. Blanch the smaller claw for 1 minute 20 seconds and the bigger claw for 1 minute 30 seconds. Cool both in ice water. Break the shells by hand or with a hammer, then peel the lobster, leaving the cartilage inside the claws. Use a pair of tweezers to remove the thin black intestine from the tail. Heat the water and whisk in the butter in small pieces. Emulsify with a stick blender.

Lobster cream
Put 35g of the cream and the lobster stock in a pan and bring to the boil. Cook the coral with the remaining 60g of cream, stirring constantly. Once it turns bright red, strain and cool. Whisk the egg yolk with the coral and add the warm liquid, whisking constantly. Process in a Thermomix at 80°C (180°F) for 5 minutes, adding the food thickener for the final minute. Strain through a cloth into a bowl set on an ice bath to obtain a light, creamy consistency.

Salad roots and leaves
Remove the outer leaves from the lettuces and discard. Cut out the roots with a knife. Remove the outer, tough skin of the roots, blanch them for 2 minutes in salted water and cool in ice water. Keep a few of the smaller leaves for this dish and use the rest for another.

Red currant sauce
Warm the red currant wine with the honey and whisk in the butter. Froth with a stick blender until a velvety texture is achieved.

Garnish
Spread out the rose petals on paper to dry them a little.

Serving
Heat the butter emulsion to approximately 55°C (130°F), add the lobster claws and leave until the cartilage can be pulled out easily. Cook the lobster for around 30 seconds in oil in a sauté pan at medium heat, then add a piece of butter and a sprig of thyme. Baste the lobster for a few seconds and remove the pan from the heat. Let the lobster rest for 20 seconds before cutting it in 2 lengthways. Glaze the 2 halves in the warm butter on both sides and drain on kitchen paper. Make 2 small smears of lobster cream on the plate, then arrange the tails and claws on the plate. Heat the salad leaves for a few seconds in a butter emulsion and sauté the roots in a warm pan. Put the leaves and roots on the plate and finally arrange the pickled rose hips around the lobster. Warm the sauce, froth it with a stick blender and add it to the plate.

BLUEBERRIES
SURROUNDED BY THEIR
NATURAL ENVIRONMENT

450g **sugar**
60g **glucose**
625g **water**
50g **blueberry purée**
200g **blueberries**
50g **spruce shoots**
3.5g **gelatine**

38g **sugar**
60g **trimoline**
120g **egg yolks**
150g **cream**
435g **full fat (whole) milk**
20g **milk powder**
2g **gelatine**
125g **spruce shoots**

145g **sugar**
525g **water**
425g **spruce shoots**
440g **sorrel**
xanthan gum

450g **full fat (whole) milk**
40g **dried yeast**
1kg **tipo '00' flour**
17g **salt**
1 **egg**
35g **sugar**
150g **butter, softened**

10 **bunches thyme** (to make 85g **when blanched**)
small bunch parsley (to make 25g **when blanched**)
110g **grapeseed oil**

28 **leaves wood sorrel**
8 **sprigs heather**
butter, for sautéing

Photograph page 136

Blueberry sorbet

Mix the sugar, glucose and water in a pan, heat to a syrup, then cool. Add the purée, the fresh berries and the spruce shoots, blend and strain. Heat a very small amount of the berry mixture. Bloom the gelatine, then dissolve into the warm mixture and add to the rest. Place in Paco containers in the refrigerator to set.

Spruce ice cream

Whisk together the sugar, trimoline and egg yolks. Heat the cream, milk and milk powder in a pan to 80°C (178°F) and pour it over the egg mixture. Pour back into the pans and cook, stirring, to make a custard. Bloom the gelatine, add and cool. When the mixture is cold, blend the spruce shoots into it and strain.

Spruce granita

Heat the water and sugar to make a syrup. Cool, blend with the spruce shoots and sorrel and pass through a fine sieve (strainer). Calculate the total weight and weigh out 0.1% of the quantity in xanthan gum. Sprinkle the xanthan into a small amount of the liquid and blend it until absorbed. Combine the 2 liquids and freeze in a deep tray. Once frozen, scrape to a powder with a fork.

Crispy brioche

Heat the milk to room temperature and dissolve the yeast in it. Add the flour, salt, eggs and sugar and mix the dough thoroughly. Add the butter while mixing and let the mixture prove (rise) for an hour. Knock back (punch down) the dough and let it prove again for an hour. Grease a loaf tin, transfer the dough to the tin and then prove again. Preheat the oven to 180°C (350°F) and bake for approximately 25 minutes. When cool, cut into 1-cm cubes.

Thyme oil

Blanch the thyme on its stems for 4–5 minutes until very tender. Cool in ice water and pull the leaves off the stems. Strain to obtain the leaves, squeeze them through a Superbag and keep dry. Pick the parsley leaves and blanch them until tender. Dry as for the thyme. Process the oil and herbs at full speed at 60°C (140°F) in a Thermomix for 12 minutes. Cool, then macerate for 24 hours. Strain through a fine cloth, applying pressure for a few hours, and keep in a squeezy bottle.

Serving

Before serving, put the plates in the freezer to get very cold. Pick the wood sorrel and heather into ice water and dry them. Sauté the brioche until crisp and golden and cool on kitchen paper (paper towels). Process the ice cream in a Pacojet, shape into balls of approximately 25mm diameter and place 3 balls of blueberry sorbet and 2 balls of spruce ice cream on each plate. Surround with 5 brioche cubes and cover everything with two and a half tablespoons of granita and a tablespoon of thyme oil. Sprinkle the wood sorrel and heather on top.

DESSERT
OF
FLOWERS

130g **double (heavy) or whipping cream**
80g **egg whites**
4g **gelatine**
75g **elderflower cordial (syrup)**
16g **sugar**
200g **skyr**

75g **pickled rose hips**
50g **sugar**
45g **water**
3g **egg white powder**
3g **gelatine**
1g **salt**

22g **sugar**
75g **water**
1 drop **violet essence**

19g **sugar**
125g **water**
2g **thyme**
0.25g **agar-agar**
5g **instant food thickener**

1 sheet **gelatine**
300g **water**
170g **sugar**
42g **glucose**
290g **skyr**
25g **lemon juice**

Any fresh **flowers in season**

Photograph page 146

Elderflower mousse
Whip the cream and the egg whites in separate bowls. Bloom the gelatine and dissolve it in a small amount of the cordial by heating it up with the sugar. Mix the cordial and the gelatine into the skyr, and fold the cream and the egg whites into it. Cut a sheet of acetate into pieces approximately 8×4cm and roll into tubes. Pipe the mousse into the tubes and freeze.

Rose hip meringue
Blend the rose hips to make a concentrate. Heat the sugar and water in a pan to 121°C (250°F). Lightly whisk the egg whites and add the caramel slowly to make an Italian meringue. Bloom the gelatine and add before the meringue base gets cold. Add the concentrate and the salt and pipe the meringues in small dots. Dry at 55°C (130°F) for 12 hours in a dehydrator.

Violet syrup
Bring the sugar and water to the boil, then cool. Add the essence and keep in a squeezy bottle.

Thyme fluid gel
Bring the sugar and water to the boil in a pan to make a syrup, then cool. Blanch the thyme and refresh it in cold water. Blend the syrup with the thyme for 1 minute at full speed and strain. Whisk the agar-agar into the liquid and bring it to the boil. When cold, blend it with a stick blender and add the instant food thickener.

Skyr sorbet
Bloom the gelatine. Warm the water, sugar and glucose and add the gelatine. Mix the rest of the ingredients and pour into Paco containers.

Garnish
Pick all the flowers off their stems and put into ice water. Dry them and keep on dry paper.

Serving
Put the plates in the freezer to get very cold. Remove the frozen mousse from the acetate tubes and let it temper to around 5°C (41°F) on a cold plate. Dot a little of the fluid gel and the syrup around the plates and cover it with meringues. Process the sorbet, make into quenelles and place a quenelle next to the mousse on each plate.

PORK NECK
AND
BULRUSHES,
VIOLETS
AND
MALT

450g **pork neck shoulder**
5 **sprigs thyme**
30g **brown butter**
40g **chicken glace**

8 **bulrushes**
40g **water**
40g **butter**

15g **malt powder**
50g **grapeseed oil**

60g **fresh cream**
1 **drop violet essence**
10–15 **wild spring violets, to garnish**

Photograph page 147

Pork
Trim the skin and excess fat off the pork neck, and wash the thyme. Vacuum-pack both with the chicken glace. Preheat a water bath to 58°C (135°F) and poach the meat for 3 hours.

Bulrushes
Trim the bulrushes down to the juicy middle part of the bottom. Heat the water and whisk in the butter to make an emulsion.

Sauce
Mix the malt powder and oil and process in a Thermomix for 3–4 minutes. Keep in a squeezy bottle, and shake every time before pouring.

Serving
Pat the pork dry with kitchen paper (paper towels) and roast it in a pan on all sides until the centre has reached 58°C (135°F). Finish the pork by adding the chicken glace to coat the entire surface of the meat. Add the bulrushes to the butter emulsion and heat in a pan for 25 seconds. Cut one slice of pork per person and put on a plate next to the bulrushes. To finish the sauce, heat the cream slowly without allowing it to boil, add the oil and violet essence without emulsifying it, and pour the sauce on to the plate alongside the pork. Garnish with the violets and serve.

WILD BLACKBERRIES
AND
SWEETCORN ICE CREAM

2 **cobs sweetcorn**
40g **brown butter**
300g **full fat (whole) milk**
14g **milk powder**
100g **cream**
30g **sugar**
30g **trimoline**
1g **salt**
70g **egg yolks**
6g **apple balsamic vinegar**

24 **cobs baby sweetcorn**
12 **fresh blackberries**

100g **very ripe wild blackberries**

liquorice

Photograph page 148

Sweetcorn ice cream

With a sharp knife cut the kernels from the sweetcorn cobs and reserve. Cut the husks into small pieces and sauté them in the brown butter until golden. Combine the milk, milk powder, cream, sugar, trimoline and salt in a pan and bring to the boil. Whisk the hot mixture into the egg yolks and return it to the pan. Cook, stirring as though making a custard, until the mixture reaches 83°C (180°F), add the sautéed husks and infuse for 24 hours. Strain the custard, add the vinegar for acidity and freeze in Paco containers. Place a flat tray in the freezer. Process the ice cream in a Pacojet and spoon into a piping (pastry) bag with a 1.5-cm nozzle (tip). Pipe a long string of ice cream on to the frozen tray and cut it into 1-cm slices. Freeze immediately.

Wild blackberries and sweetcorn

Cut half the sweetcorn into slices of approximately 6mm thick and trim the kernels off the rest. Slice the blackberries into slices of approximately 6 mm thick.

Blackberry sauce

Press the berries through a sieve (strainer) to juice them and to remove the seeds.

Serving

Put 6 slices of corn and blackberries randomly in a bowl and sprinkle the small corn kernels around. Add 6 slices of ice cream, grate a little liquorice on top and fill the gaps with blackberry sauce.

PICKLED VEGETABLES
AND
SMOKED
BONE MARROW

250g **water**
25g **dill stalks**
8g **apple balsamic vinegar**

Dill brine for the cucumbers
Blend the water, dill stalks and vinegar together and strain.

250g **water**
25g **seaweed**
30g **apple balsamic vinegar**

Seaweed brine for the kohlrabi
Blend the water, seaweed and vinegar together and strain.

125g **water**
125g **sugar**
250g **apple balsamic vinegar**
15g **apple blossom**

Apple brine for the carrots
Bring the water and sugar to the boil and cool. Add the apple vinegar and the blossom and reserve.

400g **water**
350g **rose hip vinegar**

Rose hip brine for the beetroots
Mix the water and vinegar together and reserve.

250g **water**
150g **white-wine vinegar**

White wine brine for the cauliflower
Mix the water and vinegar together and reserve.

2 **cucumbers**
3 **carrots**
1 **kohlrabi**
1 **large beetroot (beet)**
1 **cauliflower**

Pickled vegetables
Peel the cucumbers, carrots, kohlrabi and the beetroot and cut in fine slices of 1×9 cm, allowing 4–5 slices of each vegetable per person. Cut the cauliflower into small florets and slice them finely lengthways. Blanch the carrots briefly. Vacuum-pack all the vegetables with their respective pickling brine for 10 minutes. Roll all the vegetables into small tubes and reserve. Thinly slice another 4–5 slices of beetroot and kohlrabi per person, cut them into 5-cm squares and blanch them. Vacuum-pack the squares in their respective brines for 10 minutes.

2.5 kg **pork ribs, cut in small pieces**
1 **onion**
½ **apple**
2 **sticks celery**
5 **sprigs thyme**

Roast pork juice
Preheat the oven to 230°C (450°F), then roast the ribs for 30 minutes until very golden. Peel the vegetables and pan-roast them. Reduce the oven temperature to 80°C (180°F). Combine all the ingredients in a deep gastro dish and add water to cover. Cover and cook in the oven for 10 hours. Strain the liquid and reduce by half.

100g **ox marrow**
200g **water**
14g **salt**

Smoked bone marrow
Soak the marrow in ice water for 48 hours. Heat the salt and water to make a brine, and when cool soak the marrow in it for another 48 hours. Smoke lightly in a smoker with smoking chips and hay. Using a round cutter, cut the marrow into slices approximately 5mm thick. Melt the leftover marrow and strain.

20–25 **herb leaves per person from the following selection:**
yarrow
Jack-by-the-hedge
lemon verbena
white deadnettle
chickweed
tarragon
wild chervil
dill
carrot tops

Herbs
Pick all the leaves into ice water, spin them dry and keep cool.

Serving
Ensure each plate is at room temperature. Arrange all the pickled vegetable rolls around the plate, then add the squares in between the rolls. Arrange the herbs around the plate and gently heat the marrow slices. Heat the pork sauce in a pan and split it by adding a little of the marrow fat. Place some marrow slices and 2 tablespoons of the sauce on the plate.

Photograph page 149

BEETROOT
AND
RHUBARB

130g **stock syrup (50% sugar, 50% water)**
1 **leaf gelatine**
215g **beetroot (beet) juice**
8.5g **lemon juice**

50g **egg whites**
20g **sugar**
3 **leaves gelatine**
40g **yoghurt**
200g **rhubarb juice, strained**
110g **double (heavy) or whipping cream**

350g **water**
75g **sugar**
450g **sheep's milk yoghurt**
125g **cow's milk yoghurt**
7g **lemon juice**

25g **powdered freeze-dried rhubarb**

Photograph page 150

Beetroot sorbet
Heat the stock syrup. Bloom the gelatine and melt it in a little of the warm stock syrup. Combine with the rest of the ingredients and place in Paco containers to set in the freezer.

Rhubarb mousse
Whip the egg whites and sugar to a meringue and place in the refrigerator. Bloom the gelatine. Heat a little of the yoghurt and add the gelatine. Mix it with the remaining yoghurt and add the rhubarb juice. Whip the cream and fold it into the mixture, then fold in the meringues. Spoon the mousse into a square container and place in the refrigerator to set.

Yoghurt granita
Bring the water and sugar to the boil, and cool. Mix with the remaining ingredients and freeze in a metal container. When frozen solid scrape with a fork to a powder and keep in the freezer.

Serving
Put the plates and 4 round cutters of about 8cm diameter in the freezer to get very cold. For each portion, shape a small quenelle of the rhubarb mousse and roll it into the freeze-dried rhubarb powder. Process the beetroot sorbet in a Pacojet and shape a slightly bigger quenelle of it. Arrange both on a frozen plate. Fill the frozen cutter with a thin layer of the yoghurt granita, carefully remove the cutter before serving to leave a circle of granita next to the rhubarb and beetroot quenelles.

ONIONS
AND
BLUEBERRIES

8 small shallots from the island of Læsø
200g **blueberry juice**
110g **apple balsamic vinegar**
90g **honey**
2 **sprigs thyme**

4 **white onions**

300g **blueberries**
20g **sugar**
10g **apple balsamic vinegar**
salt

40g **parsley**
150g **spruce shoots**
150g **grapeseed oil**

a little butter
a few spruce shoots

Photograph page 152

Pickled shallots
Peel and halve the onions and blanch them briefly in salted water. When cool, separate the layers. Put all the remaining ingredients in a pan, bring to the boil and pour over the onions. Marinate for at least a week before using.

Onions
Peel and halve the onions and separate the layers. Blanch them briefly in salted water.

Blueberry sauce
Mash the blueberries with the sugar and add the vinegar. Vacuum-pack this mixture and cook in a water bath at 80°C (180°F) for 20 minutes. Cool, and strain to obtain a thick sauce. Season to taste with salt and vinegar.

Spruce shoot oil
Blanch the parsley, then place in a Thermomix with the spruce shoots and oil and process for 8–9 minutes on full speed. Cool, then macerate for 24 hours before straining through a cloth.

Serving
Warm the onions in a little butter, and the pickled onions in a little of their liquid. Heat the blueberry sauce slightly and pour it into the centre of the plate. Arrange the onions and pickled onions around the sauce together with the spruce oil, and finally add a few spruce shoots.

HERB TOAST WITH TURBOT ROE

2 ciabatta-style loaves
butter
salt

400g **turbot roe**
salt
20g **hay**
50g **birch wood chips**
20g **lemon juice, plus extra to taste**
400g **grapeseed oil**
water

60g **maltodextrine**
18g **vinegar powder**
10g **salt**

wild chervil
chervil
rocket (arugula) flowers
rose cress
winter cress

Photograph page 153

Toast

Freeze the loaves for a few hours. Preheat the oven to 160°C (325°F). Cut the loaves horizontally lengthways while still half frozen, then cut each slice in half to obtain 4 pieces, each approximately 2×10cm. Using foil, create 5 thin, rigid rolls the same length as the baking tray you intend to use. Lay two of the rolls a few centimetres apart on the base of the tray and place the slices of bread on top of them. Spray with plenty of melted butter and sprinkle with salt. Lay the three remaining foil rolls on top of the slices of bread, ensuring that the bread moulds itself around the rolls and into a wave-like shape. Bake for 6 minutes, then turn the tray round and bake for another 6 minutes.

Turbot roe emulsion

Sprinkle the roe with salt and let it cure for 24 hours. Smoke the roe by heating it slowly on a slotted gastro tray with the hay and chips in a smoker for around 35 minutes, then pass it through a fine sieve (strainer) and store in the refrigerator. Put the roe and the lemon juice in a mixing bowl and start whisking. While whisking at high speed gradually add the oil to emulsify the mixture like a mayonnaise. Season with more salt and lemon juice to taste, and lighten the consistency with the water if needed. Keep in a squeezy bottle on ice.

Vinegar powder

Mix everything together and store in an airtight container.

Flowers and herbs

Pick all the herbs and wash them in ice water for a few minutes. Spin them in a salad spinner and arrange 14–15 pieces per toast in small containers.

Serving

Pipe 11 dots of turbot roe emulsion on to the toast and arrange all the little picked herbs on top of the dots. Sprinkle with the vinegar powder.

SEA BUCKTHORN
AND
BEETROOT
FLØDEBOLLER

140g **beetroot (beet) juice**
119g **sugar**
72g **glucose**
15g **egg white powder**

4g **pectin**
181g **sugar**
165g **beetroot (beet) juice**
40g **glucose**
1g **citric acid**

120g **plain (all-purpose) flour**
4g **malt flour**
65g **sugar**
pinch of salt
100g **butter, softened, plus extra for greasing**
18g **egg yolks**

200g **couverture chocolate**
20g **powdered cocoa butter**

230g **water**
145g **sugar**
85g **glucose**
265g **sea buckthorn juice**
35g **egg white powder**
2 **sheets gelatine**

Photograph page 154

Beetroot meringue
Measure out 95g of the beetroot juice, bring to the boil in a pan and cool. In another pan, heat the remaining beetroot juice, 112g of the sugar and all the glucose until it forms a caramel at 117°C (242°F). Add the remaining sugar and the egg white powder to the cold beetroot juice and whisk with the caramel to make an Italian meringue.

Beetroot gel
Mix the pectin with 16g sugar. Add the beetroot juice to the glucose in a pan and dissolve the remaining 165g sugar into the mixture. Add the the pectin and sugar mixture and cook until the temperature reaches 106°C (223°F), then add the acid. Pour into containers, cool in the refrigerator and cut into 2-mm dice.

Malt biscuits (cookies)
In a large bowl, slowly incorporate the flour, malt flour, sugar and salt into the butter until well mixed. Add the egg yolks and mix to a dough with a spatula. Preheat the oven to 170°C (340°F) and grease a baking tray. Roll out the dough on a floured suface and cut into 2-cm rounds. Bake for 10 minutes.

Chocolate glaze
Melt the chocolate and cocoa butter in a double boiler and bring the temperature up to 50°C (120°F). Temper it to 27°C (80°F) and take it back up to 30°C (86°F). Tempering a larger quantity of chocolate than stated in the recipe will make the job a lot easier.

Sea buckthorn meringue
Put 65g of the water, 120g of the sugar and all the glucose in a pan and heat to 121°C (250°F) to make a syrup. Heat the sea buckthorn juice in a pan and cook until reduced to 65g, then cool. Put the remaining water and sugar with the egg white powder in a large bowl and whisk to soft peaks. Whisk in the syrup to make an Italian meringue. Bloom the gelatine and add to the mixture while still warm. Finally, add the reduced sea buckthorn juice.

Assembly
When the biscuits have baked and cooled, place them a few centimetres apart on a perforated tray. For the beet version, fold the gel into the beetroot meringue, fill a piping (pastry) bag, pipe a little on each biscuit and refrigerate. For the sea buckthorn version, follow the same procedure with the sea buckthorn but without adding gels. When cold, cover the flødeboller with the chocolate mixture and cool in the refrigerator until serving.

Flødeboller are a very traditional sweet in Denmark, consisting of a very sweet meringue covered with chocolate. They are often served for birthdays or other celebrations.

SQUID
AND
MARINATED SEASHORE HERBS, PICKLED
KOHLRABI
AND
PARSLEY

1 **Danish squid**

625g **water**
75g **apple balsamic vinegar**
65g **sea lettuce**
1 **kohlrabi**

1 **bunch parsley**
grapeseed oil

260g **spinach**

4 **small Ratte potatoes**
oil, for deep frying

Selection of seashore herbs in season
salt

Photograph page 155

Squid

Remove the body from the head. Cut the body open and scrape on both sides with a knife to clean it. Freeze the squid, and when frozen cut into portions of 6×3cm. Cut each portion into 20 equal dice and combine the dice together to re-form the 6×3cm portion.

Pickled kohlrabi

Combine the water, vinegar and sea lettuce and process in a Thermomix for 1 minute on full speed. Strain the liquid and reserve. Cut the kohlrabi in long strips and vacuum-pack it with the liquid for 10 minutes.

Parsley oil

Pick the leaves from the stems and blanch the leaves tender. Squeeze through a Superbag to remove the remaining water, keep dry on kitchen paper (paper towels). When fully dry, weigh and add the equivalent weight of the grapeseed oil. Process at full speed at 60°C (140°F) in a Thermomix for 12 minutes. Cool, then macerate for 24 hours. Strain through a fine cloth, applying pressure for a few hours.

Spinach pureé

Wash the spinach and blanch for 2–3 minutes until tender. Squeeze out all the water and freeze in Paco containers. Process the purée in the Pacojet twice and push through a cloth. Store in a squeezy bottle.

Potato crisps (chips)

Slice the potatoes with a Japanese turning vegetable slicer and fry in hot oil. Drain on kitchen paper before serving.

Seashore herbs

Pick the herbs and put into ice water, removing any insects and woody bits of stem.

Serving

Put the plates in the refrigerator to get cold. Put a small square of squid in the centre of each plate and sprinkle with salt. Roll up the bands of kohlrabi and arrange around the squid. Pipe small dots of the spinach purée on to the plate and add the seashore herbs and a few potato crisps. Mix a tablespoon of the pickling liquid with an equal amount of parsley oil and drizzle this sauce on to the plate.

SAVOURY COOKIES
WITH
SPECK
AND
BLACKCURRANTS

100g **butter**
100g **isomalt**
75g **plain (all-purpose) flour**
25g **rye flour**
4g **baking powder**
2g **salt**
5g **vinegar powder**
1 **egg, beaten**

250g **smoked speck**

2 **big leaves sorrel**
15g **freeze-dried blackcurrants**
4 **spruce shoots**

Photograph page 158

Cookies
Warm the butter to soften it. Grind the isomalt to a fine powder and strain on to the butter. Whisk the mixture until white and airy, then fold through the 2 types of flour, the baking powder , salt and vinegar powder. Finally add the egg and mix in. Leave the dough to rest overnight in the refrigerator. The next day, roll out the dough on a floured surface into 3-mm-thick sheets and freeze. Preheat the oven to 170°C (340°F). Cut out discs of 45mm diameter and bake for 6 minutes. Cool, and trim the edges by recutting the cookies to 42mm diameter.

Smoked speck
Boil the speck for 2 hours to tenderize it, and cool on a flat tray. Freeze, then slice while still frozen and cut into discs of 40mm diameter. Store between sheets of baking (parchment) paper.

Garnish
Rinse the sorrel and cut out a roughly circular piece of 40mm diameter per person. Grind the blackcurrants to a fine powder and store in an airtight container.

Serving
Place a disc of speck on a disc of sorrel and cover one of the sides in blackcurrant powder. Stand the double disc on a cookie, add a spruce shoot on top and serve.

BEETROOT GRANITA AND WOODRUFF MOUSSE

45g **pickled *Rugosa* rose leaves**
350g **beetroot (beet) juice**
5g **rose hip vinegar**
10g **stock syrup (50% sugar, 50% water)**
15g **lemon juice**

1 **sheet gelatine**
50g **egg whites**
33g **sugar**
6g **dried woodruff or 12g fresh**
150g **crème fraîche (18% fat)**
70g **double (heavy) or whipping cream**

100g **glucose**
110g **fondant powder**
5g **butter**
15g **dried rose hips**

liquorice, for grating

Photograph page 159

Beetroot granita

Soak the rose leaves in the beetroot juice for 24 hours. Mix with all the other ingredients and process for 30 seconds in a Thermomix. Pour into a metal container and freeze. When frozen, scrape to a powder with a fork and store in the freezer until needed.

Woodruff mousse

Bloom the gelatine. Whisk the egg whites with the sugar until airy. Finely powder the woodruff and add it to the crème fraîche. Heat a very small amount of the cream with the gelatine to melt it, and whisk the rest to soft peaks. Add the melted gelatine to the crème fraîche and fold in the cream and egg whites. Spread the mousse on trays to a depth of about 1cm and freeze. When frozen, cut rounds of approximately 6cm diameter and then cut these in half. Keep in the freezer until serving.

Nougatine

Heat the glucose and fondant powder in a pan to 135°C (275°F), stirring constantly, then add the butter. Spread the mixture on a silpat to cool, and when cold add the dried rose hips and process to a fine powder. Preheat the oven to 170°C (340°F). Sift the powder on to a silpat in a thin layer. Mark out rings of 6cm diameter and halve them. Bake for 3 minutes until transparent.

Serving

Put 4 round cutters of about 8cm diameter in the freezer to get very cold. Put the plates in the refrigerator to get cold. For each portion, put some mousse on a cold plate and let it defrost for 20 minutes in the refrigerator. Put the frozen round cutter around one of the half-rounds of mousse and fill the other half of the cutter with the granita. Grate some liquorice over the granita. Carefully remove the cutter, then cover the mousse with the nougatine sheet and serve.

SEA URCHIN
AND
ELDERBERRIES,
ROSE HIPS
AND
VINEGAR

4 sea urchins

360g **very ripe elderberries**
apple balsamic vinegar

4 **rose hips**
100g **water**
45g **honey**
55g **rose hip vinegar**
10g **apple balsamic vinegar**

Photograph page 160

Sea urchins
Wearing gloves, use scissors to cut carefully into the bottom of
each sea urchin and work towards the sides. Cut all the way around
the shell, taking care not to prick your fingers on the sharp spines,
and remove the bottom. Rinse the insides of the sea urchins with
cold water and remove the edible orange 'tongues' with a small
teaspoon. Clean off any impurities and store the 'tongues' on ice
in the refrigerator.

Elderberry juice
Pick the berries from the bunches and vacuum-pack them. Steam
at 80°C (180°F) for 20 minutes, then strain. Push as much of the
berries as possible through the sieve (strainer) to leave the liquid
fairly thick. Add extra vinegar to increase the acidity if necessary.

Rose hips
Cut the tops off the rose hips and then halve them. Pull out all the
seeds, then blanch the hips for a few seconds in unsalted water.
Leave to cool. Bring the water to the boil with the honey and vinegars,
and pour the result over the cooled berries. Let them marinate for
at least a week before serving.

Serving
Pour a few tablespoons of the sauce into the middle of a serving
plate and arrange the half rose hips and sea urchins on top. Add
a few elderberries and serve.

WALNUTS
AND
DRIED
BERRIES

275g **walnuts**
50g **milk**
2g **sorbet stabilizer**
135g **cream**
115g **trimoline**
65g **sugar**
10g **maltodextrine**
2g **salt**

45g **walnuts**
30g **maltodextrine**
5g **walnut oil**
7g **icing (confectioners') sugar**
1g **salt**

50g **freeze-dried blackberries**

250g **milk**
250g **cream**

Photograph page 168

Walnut ice
Blanch the walnuts 4 times in boiling water, then cool in ice water. Heat half the milk and add the sorbet stabilizer. Process all the other ingredients in a Thermomix and then combine with the walnuts and the milk mixture. Pass through a fine cloth and freeze in Paco containers.

Walnut powder
Preheat the oven to 160°C (325°F). Blanch the walnuts 4 times and dry them in the oven for 30 minutes. Process in a Thermomix to a smooth purée. When cool, whisk in the other ingredients.

Dried berries
Dip the berries in liquid nitrogen for a few seconds and then process them to a rough powder in a Thermomix. If frozen before blending the berries will stay dry; otherwise they may stick together and go soft.

Frozen milk
Put the milk and cream in a bowl and create a foam with an immmersion blender. Let the excess liquid in the foam sink for 30 seconds, then scoop it off into the liquid nitrogen in order to freeze it. Crush the frozen 'clouds' into a coarse powder and store in the freezer.

Serving
Put the plates in the freezer to get very cold. Spin the walnut ice in a Pacojet and place a few scoops in the middle of a frozen plate. Drop the frozen milk briefly in the liquid nitrogen, then sprinkle it on top of the walnut ice along with the berry powder and walnut powder.

PIG TAILS
AND
POTATO SKINS, CEP OIL
AND
WOOD CHIPS

½ leek
½ carrot
2 onions
2 sticks celery
5 sprigs thyme
butter, for sautéing
4 pig tails
5g dried verbena leaves
1 litre light chicken stock
1 bottle dark beer

8 small Vitelote potatoes
4 small white potatoes
3 handfuls hay
8g applewood chips
200g water
125g butter

200g cep (fresh porcini) trimmings
115g grapeseed oil

750g button (white) mushrooms
½ onion
½ leek
½ carrot
butter, for sautéing
750g light chicken stock
2.25kg water
6 egg whites
100g birch wine, reduced by ⅔
20g applewood chips

30g dried mushrooms

Photograph page 172

Pig tails

Peel all the vegetables, chop roughly along with the thyme and sauté them in butter in a pan. Preheat the oven to 80°C (180°F). Combine the vegetables with the tails, verbena leaves, chicken stock and beer in a gastro and cover with clingfilm (plastic wrap). Cook in the oven for 10 hours. Strain the tails and reduce the bouillon to a glace-like consistency. While still warm make an incision in the tails and pull out the bones. Let the tails cool spread out flat. Sauté the tails in butter, skin side down, at low heat until very crisp, then add the glace to the pan and glaze the tails on all sides.

Potatoes

Preheat the oven to 160°C (325°F). Rinse the unpeeled potatoes and put them in a gastro. Cover them completely with hay and bake in the oven for 20 minutes. After cooking cover the potatoes with a damp cloth and let them rest in the hay. When cold cut them in half and scoop out the middles. Toast the applewood chips in a pan to release the aromas and pour the water over them. Let it infuse for 7–8 minutes, then strain, discarding the wood. Heat the liquid and whisk in the butter to emulsify it.

Cep oil

Place the cep trimmings in a metal container and pour the oil on to them. Wrap the container tightly in clingfilm and cook it in a water bath at 80°C (180°F) for 12 hours. Strain through a cloth, pour into a small squeezy bottle and keep refrigerated.

Mushroom bouillon

Chop all the vegetables roughly. Sauté in butter in small batches, add the stock and water and boil for 1 hour. Strain the bouillon, reduce by half and cool. Lightly whisk the egg whites, add to the bouillon and heat slowly to clarify. Strain through a cloth and reduce to a quarter. Toast the wood chips in a pan to release the aromas and pour the bouillon over them. Let it infuse for 5–8 minutes, then strain the bouillon and add the birch wine to taste.

Mushroom powder

Process the dried mushrooms finely, then strain.

Serving

Heat the potatoes in the butter emulsion. Slice the pig tails into 3 pieces per person and place them on a warm plate. Arrange the potatoes around the meat, split the mushroom bouillon with the cep oil and pour 2–3 tablespoons on to the plate. Sprinkle the mushroom powder on top and serve.

LANGOUSTINES
AND
SEA
FLAVOURS

8 langoustines, approximately 150g each

100g **oysters**
18g **parsley**
150g **grapeseed oil**
lemon juice

25g **dried dulse (söl)**

100g **rye bread**
butter, for frying

butter, for sautéing

Photograph page 173

Langoustines

Remove the legs from the langoustines and discard. Break off the 2 outer pieces from the tip of the tail to release the flesh. Crack the shell surrounding the tail in your hand and peel it off in small pieces until you can pull out the flesh. Turn the peeled tail around and with a small pair of tweezers pull out the thin black intestine from the back of the tip.

Oyster emulsion

Carefully open all the oysters with an oyster knife, strain off and reserve the liquid, and put the flesh into a Thermomix bowl. Rinse the parsley, chop roughly and add to the contents of the Thermomix. Processing at full speed, add the oil slowly to emulsify, as if for a mayonnaise. If the consistency is too thick add a little oyster juice. Season to taste with the lemon juice. Strain, and keep on ice in a squeeze bottle with a small tip.

Dried dulse

Dry the dulse further by heating it at 60°C (140°F) for 3–4 hours. Process to a fine powder in the Thermomix and keep in an airtight container.

Rye bread crumble

Grate the rye bread into crumbs and store in the freezer. Before serving, fry the bread in a pan with plenty of butter until very crisp. Strain into a metal container and dry on kitchen paper (paper towels).

Serving

Place 6–7 dots of the oyster emulsion on a stone of a suitably large size, sprinkle a few rye breadcrumbs on each dot and half-cover the stone with the dried seaweed. Sauté the langoustines at high heat on one side for about 30 seconds, then add a piece of butter, turn and sauté for another 2 seconds. Place the langoustines on the stone. This dish should be eaten with fingers, so each diner should be given a warm, moist napkin with which to clean their hands.

SCALLOPS
AND
SEA URCHINS,
SEA BUCKTHORN
AND
MUIKKO

7 **Norwegian scallops in the shell**
salt
sugar

20 **sea urchins**
lemon juice
salt

16 **sea buckthorn berries**
20 **small muikko (small smoked and pickled fish from Finland)**
salt flakes
cold-pressed rapeseed (canola) oil

Photograph page 174

Scallops
Shuck the scallops carefully with a strong, pointed knife and cut around the main muscle to release them from the shell. Rinse in cold water. Sprinkle the scallops with salt and a little sugar, then place in the refrigerator for 24 hours to cure. Slice each scallop into 3 and put 5 slices on each plate. Keep the plates in the refrigerator until serving.

Sea urchin sauce
Wearing gloves, use strong scissors to cut carefully into the bottom of each sea urchin and work towards the sides. Cut all the way around the shell, taking care not to prick your fingers on the sharp spikes, and remove the bottom. Strain the juice and reserve it in the refrigerator. Rinse the insides of the sea urchins with cold water and remove the edible orange 'tongues' with a small teaspoon. Clean off any impurities and freeze the sea urchin 'tongues' in a Paco container. When frozen, spin them to a purée 2 – 3 times in the Pacojet and then let the purée defrost. Pass the sauce through a fine sieve (strainer), season it with lemon juice and salt to taste and add enough of the reserved natural juices to give a sabayon-like consistency.

Serving
Remove the plates from the refrigerator and arrange the berries and muikko around the scallops. Sprinkle a few flakes of salt on to the scallop slices. Finally pour some sauce on to each plate and add a few drops of rapeseed oil.

GLAZED BEETROOT AND APPLES

2kg **big beetroot (beet)**
20g **fresh or dried woodruff**
1 **star anise**
15g **chicken glace**
apple balsamic vinegar

200g **veal bone marrow**
70g **salt**
1 kg **water**
100g **wood chips**

4 **medium long beetroot (beet)**
4 **Mutzu apples**
60g **water**
50g **butter**
2 **sprigs thyme**
1 **large round beetroot (beet)**
8 **leaves sorrel**

Photograph page 175

Sauce
Peel and juice the big beetroot, add the woodruff and star anise and reduce to a quarter. Season with the chicken glace and vinegar and strain.

Smoked bone marrow
Soak the bone marrow in ice water for 48 hours, changing the water at least twice a day. Heat the salt and water to make a brine, cool, then soak the marrow in it for another 48 hours. Smoke lightly in a smoker with wood chips and hay for 10 minutes. Cut into slices about 5mm thick and trim into rounds with a cutter. Melt all the marrow trimmings and strain.

Garnish
Boil the long beetroot for 35 minutes or until tender, strain and peel before they cool. Cut into 1-cm discs. Slice the apples 1cm thick and trim with a round cutter to the same size as the beetroot. Heat the water and whisk in the butter in pieces to emulsify. Add the thyme and the apples and cook on low heat for around 2 minutes. Slice the large beetroot finely on a meat slicer or mandolin, then use a round cutter to cut out 3 discs per person twice the size of the beetroot and apples. Cut the sorrel leaves to the same size and leave in cold water for 5 minutes.

Serving
Preheat the oven to 160°C (325°F). Heat and glaze the beetroot in the sauce and plate them with the apples, sorrel leaves and raw beetroot discs. Heat the marrow rounds for 1 minute on a tray in the oven and add to the plate. Split the warm beetroot sauce with the melted marrow and pour this sauce on to the plate.

RED NUANCES OF LOBSTER

250g **red onions**
200g **rose hip vinegar**
100g **water**

2 **whole, live lobsters, approximately** 600g **each**
125g **water**
100g **butter**

500g **lobster stock**
75g **red beetroot (beet) juice**
10g **cornflour (cornstarch)**

95g **cream**
80g **lobster stock**
25g **fresh egg yolk**
20g **lobster coral**
6g **instant food thickener**

10 **small red beetroot (beet) with stems**
4 **stems red currants**
50g **elderberries**
12 *Rugosa* **rose petals pickled in apple balsamic vinegar**
60g **fresh dulse (söl)**
40g **radicchio**

oil, for sautéing
butter, for sautéing
sprig thyme
reduced beetroot (beet) juice, for glazing

Photograph page 176

Pickled red onions

Peel the onions and cut in quarters. Blanch for 30 seconds, and cool in ice water. Mix the vinegar and water, heat and pour over the onions. Marinade for at least 3 days before using.

Lobster

Push the tip of a strong, sharp knife through the centre of the cross on the lobster's head, cutting all the way through to the chopping board. Remove the head and tail from the body and break off both claws. Remove the knuckles from the claws and reserve for the sauce. Remove any coral from the tail, blanch it for 30 seconds, then cool in ice water. Blanch the smaller claw for 80 seconds and the bigger claw for 90 seconds. Cool both in ice water. Break the shells by hand or with a hammer, then peel the lobster, leaving the cartilage inside the claws. Use a pair of tweezers to remove the thin black intestine from the tail. Heat the water and whisk in the butter in small pieces. Emulsify with a stick blender.

Lobster sauce

Reduce the lobster stock to a quarter, add the beetroot juice and bring to the boil. Dissolve the cornflour in a tablespoon of water and whisk it into the boiling sauce.

Lobster cream

Put 35g of the cream and the lobster stock in a pan and bring to the boil. Cook the coral with the remaining 60g of cream, stirring constantly. Once it turns bright red, strain and cool. Whisk the egg yolk with the coral and add the warm liquid, whisking constantly. Process in a Thermomix at 80°C (180°F) for 5 minutes, adding the food thickener for the final minute. Strain through a cloth into a bowl set on an ice bath to obtain a light, creamy consistency.

Garnish

Cut the stems off the beetroot and reserve. Cook half the beetroot in boiling water for 40 minutes. Once cooked, peel and cut each in half. Keep them cool. Peel the raw beetroot and cut them very thinly on a mandolin into ice water. Remove the stringy parts from the stems and cut them into 9-cm lengths. Remove the red currants from their stems and keep dry. Wash the elderberries and keep dry. Spread out the pickled petals on baking (parchment) paper. Soften the dulse in water for 5 minutes and then spread out on baking paper. Wash the radicchio and spin dry.

Serving

Heat the butter emulsion to 55°C (130°F), add the lobster claws and leave until the cartilage can be easily pulled out. Cook the lobster in oil in a sauté pan at medium heat for 30 seconds, then add a piece of butter and the thyme. Baste the lobster for a few seconds and then let it rest for 20 seconds before cutting it in 2 lengthways. Glaze the 2 halves in the warm butter and drain on paper. Make a small smear of lobster cream on the plate, then arrange the tails and claws on the plate. Glaze the beetroot in reduced beetroot juice, warm the beetroot stems in butter emulsion, and warm the pickled onions in a small amount of the pickle. Arrange the cooked and raw beetroot, the stems and the dulse around the lobster. Finish by adding the berries, petals and radicchio. Warm the sauce together with the butter from the lobster pan, and plate.

ESSENTIAL PICKLES

1 kg **de-flowered ramsons (wild garlic) buds**
300g **salt**
1 litre **apple balsamic vinegar**

1 kg **immature elderberries**
300g **salt**
1 litre **apple balsamic vinegar**

350 g **elderflowers**
1 litre **apple cider vinegar**

600g ***Rugosa* roses**
1 litre **apple balsamic vinegar**

Photograph page 177

Ramsons capers
Timing is very important, the ramsons buds must be picked when their petals have dropped, but before they start to dry out. Wash the buds carefully and mix them with the salt. Leave them in the salt for 3 weeks, mixing occasionally. Rinse the salt from the buds and vacuum-pack them with the vinegar. They will be ready for use after 6 weeks.

Elderberry capers
The berries must be picked while still immature but after their stems have turned red or purple. At this point they will have developed their characteristic fruity flavour. Wash the berries carefully and mix with the salt. Leave them in the salt for 3 weeks, mixing occasionally. Rinse the salt from the elderberries and vacuum-pack with the vinegar. They will be ready for use in 6 weeks.

Pickled elderflowers
Only pick and use fully developed flowers and rinse them thoroughly to remove any insects. Vacuum-pack the flowers in bags with the vinegar. They will be ready for use in 6 weeks

Pickled rose flowers
Make sure there are no bugs in between the rose petals, mix the roses with the vinegar, and vacuum-pack in bags. They will be ready for use in 4 weeks. The pickling will mellow the roses' natural bitterness and accentuate their flavour.

A fundamental part of the approach to produce at Noma consists of the pickling of produce when it is at its best and using it as a flavouring for the rest of the year. The four pickling guides listed here are the most essential, and at Noma the end products are as important as salt. They will all keep in the refrigerator for 1–2 years.

CARROTS
AND
BUTTERMILK

500g **peeled and sliced carrots**
800g **fresh carrot juice**

375g **carrot purée**
500g **fresh carrot juice**
25g **lemon juice**
70g **orange juice**
70g **stock syrup (50% sugar, 50% water)**
3 **leaves gelatine**
4g **sorbet stabilizer**
3g **maltodextrin**
40g **apple balsamic vinegar**

4 **leaves gelatine**
350g **buttermilk**
100g **whey**
75g **cream**
75g **stock syrup**
12g **lemon juice**

75g **egg**
90g **egg whites**
70g **plain (all-purpose) flour**
75g **sugar**
2g **powdered malt**
15g **liquorice powder**
1.5g **salt**

1 **litre carrot juice**
apple balsamic vinegar
4 **carrots**
8 **baby carrots**

Photograph page 178

Carrot purée
Put the carrots and juice in a large pan and cook until all the juice has evaporated. Process in a Thermomix to a smooth purée, then cool.

Carrot sorbet
Mix the carrot purée with the carrot juice, lemon juice, orange juice and stock syrup. Bloom the gelatine. Heat a small amount of the mixture with the stabilizer and maltodextrin and melt the gelatine in it. Mix with the main batch and add the vinegar. Freeze in Paco containers.

Buttermilk foam
Bloom the gelatine. Mix together the buttermilk, whey, cream, stock syrup and lemon juice, then heat up a small amount of the mixture with the gelatine. Add to the rest of the mixture and pour into a siphon bottle. Cool, and when set add 2 cartridges and shake.

Liquorice sponge
Preheat the oven to 170°C (340°F) and grease a 15-cm cake tin. Beat the eggs together in a large bowl, then fold in the remaining ingredients. Pour into the baking tin and bake for 15 minutes. Cool on a rack, then break the cake into smaller pieces. Preheat the oven to 60°C (140°F) and dry the cake in it on a tray for 12 hours.

Garnish
Reduce the carrot juice to one-tenth of its original volume and season with the vinegar. Thinly slice all the regular-size carrots sideways and soak a third of them in ice water. Strain, then vacuum-pack them with the carrot juice for 6 minutes. Blanch the rest of the regular-size carrots and vacuum-pack them the same way for 6 minutes. Preheat the oven to 70°C (160°F). Dry half of the blanched carrots and half of the marinated carrots on trays in the oven for 12 hours. Cut the long thin roots off the baby carrots and pick the green leaves from the tops. Use the main part of the baby carrots for another dish.

Serving
Process the sorbet in a Pacojet and, using a size 40 ice cream scoop, place a round ball of sorbet on to the middle of each plate. Shake the siphon vigorously and cover the sorbet in buttermilk foam. Arrange the different types of sliced carrots, the dried liquorice sponge and the carrot tops around the plates.

For this dessert it is essential that the carrots used are of a very high quality and freshly harvested. At Noma we use biodynamically grown carrots from Kiselgården.

SWEET SHRIMP FROM SMÖGEN, FROZEN RED CURRANT JUICE

20 raw shrimp

200g **red currant juice**

240g **dill**
180g **grapeseed oil**

45g **cream**
25g **milk**
70g **dill oil**

40g **white bread**
butter, for frying
1 small bunch tarragon
1 small bunch dill

salt

Photograph page 179

Shrimp
Shell the shrimp carefully, starting at the tail end and working towards the head. Line up the shelled shrimp on a plate and refrigerate.

Red currant granita
Add water to the red currant juice until the sugar content reaches 12° on a refractometer. Freeze in containers, and when frozen scrape to a powder with a fork.

Dill oil
Pick the dill leaves off the stems and blanch for 5 minutes in salted water. Cool in ice water and dry completely on paper. Add the oil and process in a Thermomix at 80°C (180°F).

Cream and dill oil
Mix all the ingredients and keep in the refrigerator until about 5 minutes before serving.

Garnish
Reduce the bread to small crumbs, fry in butter and cool. Pick the herbs into ice water, then dry.

Serving
Take the cold plate of shrimp out of the refrigerator as late as possible. Sprinkle the herbs and fried breadcrumbs on top, then add the cream and dill oil and the granita. Finally sprinkle salt over the granita and prawns.

PUMPKIN AND MARINATED HERRING, WALNUT JUICE

2 **Hokkaido pumpkins**
25g **dulse (söl)**
250g **water**
30g **apple balsamic vinegar**
15g **walnut oil**

2 **small fresh herrings**
350g **coarse sea salt**
175g **rose hip vinegar**
200g **water**

125g **walnuts**
125g **water**

flakes of salt

Photograph page 182

Pumpkin

Peel the pumpkins and slice them finely. Blanch lightly in salted water, then cool. Mix the remaining ingredients in the bowl of a Thermomix and process for 1 minute. Strain through a fine cloth and add to the pumpkins. Vacuum-pack for 6 minutes, then discard the liquid.

Herrings

Scale and bone the herrings, and cover the resulting fillets with the salt. Cure the fish for 2 hours in the refrigerator. Rinse off the salt, then vacuum-pack the fish with the vinegar and water for 10 minutes.

Walnut juice

Preheat the oven to 160°C (325°F). Blanch the walnuts in boiling water 3 times, then toast in the oven for 15 minutes or until golden. When cooled blend them with the water and let the mixture macerate for 24 hours in the refrigerator. Pass the mixture through a Superbag to obtain the juice.

Serving

Roll up the slices of pumpkin and the herring fillets and put on a plate. Sprinkle with flakes of salt and add 2 tablespoons of the walnut juice to each serving.

GRILLED LAMB SHANK
AND
RAMSONS LEAVES, YELLOW BEETROOT
AND
ELDERFLOWERS

4 small lamb shanks
50g **chicken glace**
25g **large ramsons (wild garlic) leaves**

30 **small yellow beetroots (beets)**

350g **large yellow beetroot (beet)**
salt
apple balsamic vinegar

1 **bunch elderflower blossom**

60g **elderflower cordial (syrup)**
a little butter

Photograph page 183

Lamb shank
Vacuum-pack the shanks with the chicken glace and ramsons and cook them at 63°C (145°F) for 24 hours.

Beetroot
Divide the beetroot into 2 groups by size. Cook the smaller group in water until tender and then peel. Peel the bigger group and slice finely on a mandolin. Keep in ice water for 10 minutes to crisp them, then dry.

Sauce
Peel the beetroot, juice in a juicer and then reduce the juice to one-third. Pour all the juices from the bags containing the cooked lamb shanks into a bowl and add a few tablespoons of the reduced beetroot juice. Season with salt and vinegar.

Garnish
Cut the flowers into smaller sprigs and keep refrigerated until serving.

Serving
Char-grill (charbroil) the lamb shanks and glaze in a few tablespoons of warm chicken glace. Place a portion of meat in the centre of each plate. Heat the cooked beetroot in a little butter and a few drops of cordial. Drop the raw beetroot into the rest of the cordial for a few seconds to sweeten. Add the raw and cooked beetroot to the plate, add the elderflowers and finally the sauce.

STONE CRAB
AND
BEACH MUSTARD, COCKLE GEL

2.5 litres **water**
1 litre **white wine**
juice of 2 **lemons**
4 **stone crabs**
10g **mayonnaise**
salt

Shells from 4 **stone crabs**
100g **shallots**
1 **green apple**
3 **sprigs thyme**
1.5 litres **water**
80g **white wine**
2 **leaves gelatine**
50g **European sea rocket**

1kg **cockles**
1 **shallot, chopped**
2 **sprigs thyme**
300g **dry white wine**
1 **leaf gelatine per** 100g **juice**

20 **beach mustard flowers**

Photograph page 184

Crabmeat
Bring the water, wine and lemon juice to the boil and pour it over the crabs. Leave for 40 minutes. Break up the crabs and crush them with a hammer to pull out all the meat. Keep the crabmeat on ice until ready to serve and reserve the coral. Sift through the meat several times to make sure no pieces of shell remain. Blend 15g of the crab coral with the mayonnaise and fold it through the meat. Season to taste with salt.

Beach mustard gel
Preheat the oven to 80°C (180°F). Chop the crab shells into pieces of approximately 5×5cm, discard the 'dead man's fingers' and toast the shells in a pan. Peel the shallots and apple and cut into dice. Caramelize the vegetables in a pan and combine with the thyme, water and wine in a deep tray. Cover the tray with clingfilm (plastic wrap) and steam in the oven for 12 hours. Strain, then reduce the liquid to half, cool and freeze in a metal container. When frozen, remove from the container and let it defrost on a cloth set over a bowl in the refrigerator to clarify it. This will take between 12 and 24 hours depending on the amount. Bloom the gelatine. Clean the sea rocket thoroughly to get rid of any sand and blend it with 200g of the clarified juice. Strain the liquid and heat a little of it with the gelatine.

Cockle gel
Put the cockles, shallots, thyme and white wine in a large warm pan and cook, covered, for 45 minutes. Strain, reduce to half, cool and freeze. When frozen, clarify as for the crab bouillon. Heat the juice slightly, weigh and add the appropriate quantity of the gelatine. Set in the refrigerator.

Garnish
Rinse the flowers, taking care not to damage the petals.

Serving
Place a bowl in the freezer to get very cold. For each person, fashion an 18g-ball of crab mixture and place on the plate. Lightly mix equal amounts of the 2 gels in the ice-cold bowl and place around the crab. Add the flowers and serve.

BEETROOT
AND
AROMATIC SEEDS,
RED
GOOSEBERRIES
AND
DEWBERRIES

4 big, long beetroot (beet)

10 red gooseberries
32 dewberries

80g red beetroot (beet) juice
160g red gooseberry juice

apple balsamic vinegar
salt
angelica shoots
coriander (cilantro) shoots
lavender flowers
yarrow flowers
red onion flowers
lemon thyme
fresh seeds of wild parsnip
35g rapeseed (canola) oil

Photograph page 185

Beetroot
Cook half the beetroot in salted water for approximately 1 hour until tender, and skin them before they cool. Slice thinly on a mandolin, then cut the slices into rounds of 30 mm diameter. Peel the remaining beetroot and slice and cut them in the same way as the cooked ones.

Berries
Top and tail (trim) the gooseberries and cut them in half. Remove any stems and leaves from the dewberries.

Sauce
Mix the 2 juices and heat them to lukewarm.

Serving
Add a drop of vinegar and a sprinkle of salt to each half gooseberry. Place all the berries in a bowl and arrange the finely sliced beetroot, cooked and raw, around them. Crush the angelica and coriander shoots lightly, then sprinkle them and a selection of the flowers and herbs on top of the beetroot. Add the rapeseed oil to the lukewarm sauce, mix, add to the plate and serve.

RADISHES
IN A
POT

16 long radishes

8g **parsley**
8g **chives**
5g **tarragon**
5g **chervil**
5g **shallots**
125g **sheep's milk yoghurt**
15g **capers**
50g **mayonnaise**
5g **instant food thickener**

Day 1
175g **flour**
85g **malt flour**
50g **hazelnut flour**
25g **sugar**
75g **lager**

Day 2
40g **flour**
20g **malt flour**
50 **hazelnut flour**
4g **salt**
60g **butter, melted**

sea salt

Photograph page 186

Radishes
Wash the radishes and cut off the bottoms. Remove the leaves and stems, leaving only a few pretty ones.

Herb cream
Roughly chop the herbs and shallots. Add the yoghurt and capers and process in a Thermomix. Blend in the mayonnaise and pass through a fine sieve (strainer). Blend the mixture with the instant food thickener.

Malt soil
Day 1: Preheat the oven to 90°C (195°F). Mix all the dry ingredients in a bowl and pour into a food processor. Process 3 times in short bursts while adding the beer. Spread on a tray and dry in the oven for 3–6 hours. Push through a coarse sieve to remove the thickest lumps.

Day 2: Repeat the mixing procedure from Day 1 with the remaining malt soil ingredients, then mix the 2 batches together by hand, ensuring that no moist lumps are left in the mixture.

Serving
Use a piping (pastry) bag to half-fill a small pot with the herb cream. Season the radishes with sea salt and insert them in the cream. Sprinkle enough malt soil on top of the radishes to cover the cream completely and the radishes partially.

SHORT RIB
OF
BEEF
AND
ROSES,
MALT PUFFS
AND
BEETROOT

1 short rib of beef, approximately 1.5 kg
a little chicken glace
a few sprigs thyme

1 sheet gelatine
3g agar-agar
250g beetroot (beet) juice

100g reduced oxtail juice
50g reduced onion bouillon

300g beetroot (beet) juice
0.5g woodruff
2 giant beetroot (beet) from Gotland
2 Topaz apples

190g tipo '00' flour
2.5g fine cooking salt
10g malt
90g lager

20g cep (fresh porcini) oil
2g rose hip vinegar
1 drop rose hip essence
20 *Rugosa* rose petals
butter emulsion

Photograph page 187

Beef
Preheat the oven to 80°C (178°F). Put the meat in a cooking bag
with a tablespoon of chicken glace and a few sprigs of thyme.
Cook in the oven on slotted trays for 10 hours. Cut into 50g
portions, avoiding the fatty parts. Retrieve the juice from the
cooking bag, reduce it to a third and reserve.

Beet gel
Bloom the gelatine in cold water. Whisk the agar-agar into the
beetroot juice and bring to the boil while whisking. Add the
gelatine and set on trays. When cold, cut into 12-cm squares.

Sauce
Mix the juice and bouillon in a pan and heat.

Garnish
Heat the beetroot juice with the woodruff in a pan, reduce to a
quarter and strain. Cook one of the beetroots in water until tender,
and cool. Cut cylinder shapes approximately 6cm long from the
cooked beetroot, and both of the apples, with an apple corer.
Cut the second (raw) beetroot in fine slices, then into discs with
a round cutter.

Malt puffs
Mix the flour and salt, then add the malt and beer. Knead the dough
until homogenous, then rest for 30 minutes. Pass through a pasta
machine until 0.6 mm thick and cut into 2cm rounds. Fry at 180°C
(350°F) until puffed and crisp.

Serving
Glaze the beef in a sauté pan in its reduced cooking juices. Add the
cep oil to the sauce to split it. Glaze the beetroot cylinders in the
beetroot reduction, and season with rose hip vinegar and essence.
Cook the apples briefly in the butter emulsion. Plate 2 warm beet
cylinders and an apple cylinder on the side of each plate and partly
cover them with gel. Add 5 rose petals, a portion of meat,
4 raw beetroot slices and 2 malt puffs to each plate and drizzle
the sauce around.

THE
ONION FAMILY

10 small shallots from Læsø
100g **dark beer**
55g **apple balsamic vinegar**
45g **honey**
1 **sprig thyme**
1 **bay leaf**

10 **bunches thyme (to make** 85g **when blanched)**
small bunch parsley (to make 25g **when blanched)**
110g **grapeseed oil**

2.5kg **Zittauer onions**
1.25kg **light chicken stock**
75g **egg whites**
5g **lemon juice**
reduced birch wine or reduced white wine
salt

2½ **white salad onions or fresh onions**
grapeseed oil

100g **tapioca or sago pearls**

5–6 **different types of new onions in season**

4 **round slices of Swedish Prästost,**
2mm thick and 13cm in diameter
a few leaves Jack-by-the-hedge
salt
butter emulsion

Photograph page 188

Pickled onions
Peel the shallots and cut them in half. Blanch for 2–3 minutes until soft, then cool in ice water. When cold, cut off the bottoms and separate into single petals. Bring the remaining ingredients to the boil in a pan and pour over the shallots to pickle them. Keep for at least a week before using.

Thyme oil
Blanch the thyme on its stems for 4–5 minutes until very tender. Cool in ice water, and pull off the stems. Strain to obtain the leaves, and squeeze them through a Superbag to remove the remaining water. Keep dry on kitchen paper (paper towels). Pick the leaves from the parsley and blanch them until tender. Dry as for the thyme. Process the herbs with the oil at full speed on 60°C (140°F) in a Thermomix for 12 minutes. Cool, and macerate for 24 hours. Strain through a fine cloth, applying pressure for a few hours, and keep in a small squeezy bottle.

Onion bouillon
Peel the onions and halve them. Place in big gastro trays and add the chicken stock, then add water to cover. Wrap in clingfilm (plastic wrap), add a lid, then wrap the gastro trays in clingfilm again and steam at 90°C (195°F) for at least 30 hours. Reduce the bouillon to about half, then cool. Whisk the egg whites until slightly fluffy, add the lemon juice and whisk into the bouillon. Warm the bouillon slowly, stirring for the first few minutes. Keep heating until a 'cake' takes shape on top and the bouillon beneath is clarified. Very carefully strain the bouillon, taking care not to break up the 'cake'. Add reduced birch wine or white wine to taste and season with salt.

Onion compote
Peel the onions and slice very finely on a mandolin. In a shallow, wide-based pan, sauté them in the oil over a low heat. Cover with a circle of baking (parchment) paper to enable the onions to cook in the steam. Keep stirring them until soft and tender. Take care not to caramelize the compote too much or it will become too sweet.

Tapioca
Rinse the tapioca in plenty of water. Bring to the boil in fresh water and cook over a medium heat for 20 minutes. Strain the liquid and cool the tapioca by rinsing it in cold water.

Blanched onions
Trim and peel the onions, and blanch them briefly in salted water.

Serving
Add a few tablespoons of onion bouillon to the tapioca to give it a stew-like consistency. Warm the thyme oil and add it to the onion bouillon to split it like a vinaigrette. Heat the compote, put 15g on each plate and cover with a slice of cheese. Melt the cheese over the compote with a gas burner and season with salt. Heat the onions in a butter emulsion until piping hot, and warm the pickled ones in a small amount of the pickle. Arrange all the onions and herbs around the cheese. Serve the bouillon and the tapioca separately at the tableside.

GRILLED PEAR MARINATED IN HERB FLOWERS, DUCK LIVER AND GIZZARDS

5 bunches thyme (to make 42g when blanched)
small bunch of parsley (to make 12g when blanched)
55g grapeseed oil

2 very ripe sweet Gråpære or Grise Bonne pears
salt

70g duck liver
30g duck gizzards
25g finely chopped shallots
2g finely chopped thyme
grapeseed oil
125g dark beer
70g duck glace

thyme flowers
lavender flowers
heather flowers
rosemary flowers

Photograph page 189

Thyme oil
Blanch the thyme on its stems for 4–5 minutes until very tender. Cool in ice water and pull off the stems. Strain to obtain all the leaves and squeeze through a Superbag to remove the remaining water. Keep dry on kitchen paper (paper towels). Pick the leaves from the parsley and blanch them until tender. Dry as for the thyme. Process the oil and herbs in a Thermomix at full speed on 60°C (140°F) for 12 minutes. Cool, then macerate for 24 hours. Strain through a fine cloth, applying pressure for a few hours, and keep in a small squeezy bottle.

Grilled (broiled) pear
Peel the pears and cut in thick slices lengthways. Remove the cores and char-grill 1 slice per person on one side only. Take the pears off the heat and rub thyme oil and salt into them to taste.

Sauce
Blend the liver and gizzards to a fine purée and pass it through a fine sieve (strainer). Sauté the shallots and thyme in a little oil in a pan and add the purée. Let the mix cook for 2 minutes and add the beer. Reduce to half and add the duck glace. The consistency of the final sauce must be like that of an Italian ragù or bolognese sauce.

Serving
Warm the plates. Place a slice of pear on each plate and heat the sauce. Add the thyme flowers to the sauce and split it with plenty of thyme oil. Drizzle sauce around the pear, sprinkle with the remaining herb flowers and serve.

CELERIAC
AND
ICELANDIC MOSS, SEAWEED
AND
EGG YOLK

1 whole celeriac (celery root)
120g **Icelandic dulse (söl) or Cladonia lichen**
500g **salt**
500g **flour**
300g **water**

4 **organic eggs** approximately 55–65g **each**
65g **dried dulse (söl)**
seaweed powder, for rolling
salt

30g **apple balsamic vinegar**
25g **mustard from Gotland**
120g **cold-pressed mustard oil from Gotland**

Photograph page 191

Celeriac
Preheat the oven to 220°C (425°F). Peel the celeriac and cover with the dulse. Mix the salt, flour and water into a dough, roll it out and use it to cover the celeriac. Bake in the oven for 20 minutes, then reduce oven temperature to 160°C (325°F) and cook for another 35–45 minutes, depending on size. Cut the crust open and scoop out 4 pieces with a spoon.

Poached egg yolk and dulse
Blend the dulse into a fine powder and keep dry. Poach the eggs in a water bath for 32 minutes. Crack them open and discard the shells and whites. Roll the egg yolks in the seaweed powder and season with salt.

Vinaigrette
Mix the vinegar and mustard and emulsify the oil into the mix.

Serving
Place a piece of celeriac on each plate with a warm egg yolk next to it and the vinaigrette around it.

DANDELION
AND
NASTURTIUM, SEAKALE FRUIT
AND
YELLOW BEETROOTS

4 organic eggs, each weighing approximately 55–65g

140g **picked yellow nasturtium flowers**
20g **water**
30g **apple balsamic vinegar**
6g **Dijon mustard**
220g **grapeseed oil**

8 **medium yellow beetroots (beets)**
60g **elderflower cordial (syrup)**

32 **nasturtium berries**
8 **seakale seeds**
8 **dandelions**

a little butter

Photograph page 192

Poached eggs
Poach the eggs in a water bath at 65°C (150°F) for 35 minutes until soft poached.

Nasturtium sauce
Combine the flowers, water, vinegar and mustard and process in a Thermomix, then pour in the oil while mixing as quickly as possible. Strain the mixture through a fine cloth and keep on ice until the dish is ready to be served. Add extra vinegar to increase the acidity just before serving if necessary.

Yellow beetroots
Divide the beetroots into 2 roughly equal groups, smaller ones and larger ones. Boil the smaller ones in water and peel them. Slice and trim to approximately 2 cm diameter. Peel the larger beetroots and slice finely on a mandolin. Drop the slices into ice water for 10 minutes to crisp and dry them. Drop them in the cordial a few seconds before serving to add a little sweetness.

Garnish
Cut the berries and seeds from their stems and pick the petals from the dandelions.

Serving
Heat the eggs to 58°C (135°F) in a water bath and crack them open. Discard the egg white. Place the yolk in the middle of the plate. Warm the sauce, ensuring it does not boil or it will split. Heat the berries, seeds and cooked beetroots in a little butter and add them to the plate. Finally, add the raw beetroots, dandelions and sauce.

SNAILS
AND
MOSS

32 **snails**
6 **salad leaves (greens)**

400g **fresh organic milk**
20g **cream**
8g **buttermilk**
1.5g **rennet**

16 **Jack-by-the-hedge plants with roots**
16 **stems rose cress with roots**
12–16 **pieces moss of different types**
12 **stems yarrow**

180g **spinach**

a little butter
a little reduced chicken glace

Photograph page 202

Snails

Let the snails live off the salad leaves for 2–3 days to clean out their systems. Rinse them in plenty of water and put them in a large pan. Cover with water and bring slowly to the boil, making sure that the snails don't escape. When the water has boiled and all the snails are set firm, rinse them again and simmer them slowly in fresh salted water for 1 hour 30 minutes. Remove the pan from the heat and let the snails cool in the liquid. Reserve some of the liquid for glazing the snails later. Cut the tops off the snails and keep only the lower meaty part.

Fresh cheese

Preheat the oven to 36°C (97°F). Heat the milk in a pan to 36°C (97°F) and add the remaining ingredients. Pour into covered plastic containers and cook in the oven for 1 hour 25 minutes. Cool with the lids off.

Roots and moss

Keeping each herb attached to its roots, rinse the roots to clean them and refresh in iced water. Pick through the moss to remove any woody bits, and wash.

Spinach purée

Wash the spinach very well and blanch it for 2–3 minutes until tender. Squeeze out all the water and freeze the spinach in Paco containers. Process the spinach twice in the Pacojet and strain through a cloth. Store in a squeezy bottle.

Serving

Warm the roots for 20 seconds in a spoonful of butter in a sauté pan and heat the moss for the final 10 seconds. Sauté the snails quickly and glaze them in reduced chicken glace and the reserved cooking liquid. The aim of the presentation is to re-create the habitat of the snails: place the cheese in the middle of the plate and surround it with the snails, dots of purée, yarrow and roots.

POTATO CRISPS
WITH
ANISE
AND
CHOCOLATE

2 **Bintje potatoes**
800ml **grapeseed oil**

400g **couverture chocolate**
20g **powdered cocoa butter**
4g **green anise seeds**
4g **fennel seeds**

Photograph page 203

Potatoes

Peel the potatoes and slice them finely into cold water. Leave the slices in the cold water until the starch has rinsed out and then pat dry. Heat the oil carefully in a deep fryer to approximately 170°C (340°F) and fry the potatoes until crisp. Cool on grease-absorbent paper.

Covering and serving

Melt the chocolate and the cocoa butter and bring to 50°C (120°F). Temper it to 27°C (80°F), and then increase the temperature back up to 30°C (85°F). Pull the potatoes through the tempered chocolate to cover them completely, then cool on a tray. Sprinkle the anise and fennel seeds over the potatoes before they have cooled completely.

CHESTNUTS
AND
WALNUTS,
RYE
AND
CRESS

350g **chestnuts**
80g **walnuts**

100g **birch wine**
60g **butter**
100g **water**
60g **bleak roe from Kalix, Sweden**

50g **rye bread**
butter, for frying

80g **cress**
salt flakes

Photograph page 204

Chestnuts and walnuts
Extract the chestnuts from their shells with the tip of a small knife and peel off the hairy skin. Cut into 2-mm slices with a truffle slicer into ice water and use the trimmings for another dish. Shell the walnuts with a nutcracker. Soak the nuts in warm water, peel off the brown skin and finely chop the nuts.

Sauce
Reduce the birch wine to one-third, whisk in the butter while the reduction is still warm and add the water. Dry the bleak roe on kitchen paper (paper towels).

Rye bread
Grate the bread into crumbs, fry slowly in plenty of butter until golden, then leave to cool and drain on kitchen paper.

Serving
In the middle of each plate, lean chestnut slices up against each other to give height and volume. Avoid stacking and clumping, which would spoil the intended light appearance of the dish. Sprinkle the cress and the ryebread crumbs over the chestnuts. Heat the sauce and add the bleak roe. Drizzle sauce around and in between the chestnut slices. Finish off with a few flakes of salt and the walnuts.

SMOKED BONE MARROW
AND
ONION,
THYME FLOWERS
AND
VEAL BREAST

350g **bone marrow**
45g **salt**
700g **water**

2.5kg **Zittauer onions**
1.2kg **light chicken stock**
75g **egg whites**
5g **lemon juice**

15 bunches **thyme**
(to make approximately 125g when **blanched**)
small bunch **parsley**
(to make approximately 35g when **blanched**)
165g **grapeseed oil**

200g **veal breast**
500g **grapeseed oil**

salt flakes
20 **pickled ramsons (wild garlic) capers**
20 **small thyme flowers**

Photograph page 205

Smoked bone marrow

Soak the bone marrow in ice water for 48 hours, changing the water at least twice a day. Combine the salt and water in a large pan to make a brine, and heat until all the salt has dissolved. When cool, soak the bone marrow in the brine for another 48 hours. Smoke lightly on a slotted gastro tray in a smoker with smoking chips and hay. Cut into slices of approximately 5mm diameter, then trim them to shape with a round cutter.

Onion bouillon

Peel the onions and halve them. Place in big gastro trays, then add the chicken stock and enough water to cover. Wrap the trays in clingfilm (plastic wrap), cover with a lid, then wrap in another layer of clingfilm and steam at 90°C (195°F) for at least 30 hours. Reduce the bouillon by about half, and cool. Whisk the egg whites a little to get some air into them, then whisk them into the bouillon with the lemon juice. Warm the bouillon slowly, stirring for the first few minutes. Keep heating until a removable 'cake' of impurities forms on top and the bouillon beneath is clarified.

Thyme oil

Blanch the thyme on its stalks for 4–5 minutes until very tender. Cool in ice water, then pull off the leaves and squeeze them through a Superbag to lose the remaining water. Pat dry, and keep dry on absorbent paper for a few hours. Pull the parsley leaves from the stalks and blanch the leaves until tender. Dry as for the thyme. Process the herbs with the oil at full speed on 60°C (140°F) in a Thermomix for 12 minutes. Cool, and macerate for 24 hours. Strain through a fine cloth, applying pressure for a few hours, then keep the thyme oil in a small squeezy bottle.

Veal breast

Cook the meat in water until tender, then pull apart following the natural direction of its fibres. It is easiest to do this if you keep the meat warm and in the cooking liquid. Carefully fry the meat in the oil at 160°C (325°F) until crisp, and drain on grease-absorbent paper.

Serving

Heat the bone marrow slices in the oven, sprinkle a few flakes of salt on top and place them on the plates. Warm the bouillon and add the thyme oil to make a split sauce. Arrange the capers and flowers around the marrow and pour the sauce in between them. Add the crisp veal breast at the side. The dish is intended to be served without cutlery, just a piece of bread to mop up the juices.

HEN
OF THE
WOOD
AND
BLOOD
PURÉE

300–400g **hen-of-the-wood mushrooms in 4 pieces**
grapeseed oil, for sautéing
butter
salt

275g **fresh pig's blood**
25g **chicken glace**
25g **cream**
75g **mineral water**
2g **ground caraway seeds**
1.5g **salt**
13g **apple cider vinegar**

245g **lingonberries**
sugar

40–50 **leaves wood sorrel**
16–20 **lingonberries**

cold-pressed rapeseed (canola) oil

Photograph page 208

Mushrooms
After picking the mushrooms, leave them in the refrigerator
for 10 days to allow them to dry out a little. When dry, brush the
mushrooms free of sand and dirt and sauté them in the grapeseed
oil briefly in a pan at high heat to release the flavour of roast chicken,
which gives this mushroom its name. Add a piece of butter and
season with salt.

Blood purée
Process the blood in a Thermomix at 85°C (185°F) for 5 minutes.
Warm up the chicken glace, cream and water and add to the blood.
Pass the mixture through a sieve (strainer) and season to taste with
the caraway, salt and vinegar.

Lingonberry sauce
Press the berries through a cloth to obtain the juice. Season with
sugar to taste.

Garnish
Leave the stems on the wood sorrel leaves and rinse them in water.
Spin the leaves dry and keep them cool and dry until needed.

Serving
Heat the blood purée slightly and place a pool of it in the middle
of the plate. Warm the lingonberry juice with a few tablespoons
of rapeseed oil and pour it around the purée. Add the mushrooms,
berries and finally the wood sorrel.

VEAL TONGUE
AND
BREAST,
OXTAIL
AND
BOUILLON

70g **salt**
1kg **water**
1 **small veal tongue**
40g **chicken glace**

200g **veal breast**
500g **grapeseed oil**

1.25kg **Zittauer onions**
600g **light chicken stock**
35g **egg whites**
2g **lemon juice**

1.25kg **oxtail cut in pieces**
oil and salt, for rubbing
125g **red wine**
60g **dark beer**
600g **light chicken stock**
1 **onion, peeled and diced small**
1 **carrot, peeled and diced small**
1 **leek, peeled and thinly sliced**
small bunch thyme

1 **baby celeriac (celery root)**
4 **sticks celery**
5 **stems wild watercress**
20–25 **leaves wild baby sorrel**

apple balsamic vinegar
chicken glace
a little butter

Photograph page 212

Veal tongue

Mix the water and salt to make a brine, place the tongue in a vacuum bag filled with brine for 24 hours. Rinse the tongue and place it in a cooking bag. Cook in a water bath at 63°C (145°F) for 24 hours and then cool immediately in ice water. Peel, and cut into 50g portions.

Crunchy veal fibres

Cook the veal breast in water until tender, this should take around 2 hours. Keeping it warm and in the cooking liquid, pull it apart along its natural fibres. Carefully fry the meat in the oil in a pan at 160°C (325°F) and drain on kitchen paper (paper towels).

Onion bouillon

Peel the onions and halve them. Place in big gastro trays and add the chicken stock, then enough water to cover. Wrap in clingfilm (plasticwrap), add a lid, wrap the the gastro trays in clingfilm again and steam at 90°C (195°F) for at least 30 hours. Reduce the bouillon to approximately half, and cool. Lightly whisk the egg whites, add the lemon juice and whisk into the bouillon. Warm the bouillon slowly, stirring for the first few minutes. Keep heating until a removable 'cake' forms on top and the bouillon beneath is clarified. Continue heating until reduced to a quarter.

Oxtail bouillon

Preheat the oven to 225°C (440°F). Rub the oxtail pieces in the oil and salt and then brown them in a roasting pan in the oven, turning them from time to time to brown evenly. Reduce the oven temperature to 80°C (180°F). Combine the oxtail with the wine, beer, stock, vegetables and thyme in a deep gastro tray. Add water to cover everything and wrap the tray in clingfilm. Put a lid on top and add one more layer of clingfilm. Cook the oxtail in the oven for 6–8 hours. Strain the stock and reduce it to a quarter, reserving the meat for another dish.

Garnish

Scrub the celeriac and cut the top off. Cut into 4–6 pieces depending on size and blanch for 3–4 minutes. Clean the celery and remove the strings. Cut into 10-cm pieces and blanch for 10–15 seconds. Pick the leaves from the watercress stems, reserving the stems. Wash the sorrel leaves in ice water and keep on dry paper.

Serving

Mix the bouillons together and add extra vinegar to taste. Sear the veal tongue in a pan and finish by glazing it with chicken glace. Heat the vegetables in a little butter, adding the watercress stems for the last 10 seconds. Put the tongue on the plate surrounded by the vegetables, put the crunchy fibres on top and add the herbs. Pour oxtail sauce around the tongue.

RAZOR CLAMS
AND
PARSLEY,
HORSERADISH
AND
MUSSEL JUICE

4 big Norwegian razor clams approximately 18–20cm long
80g **baby spinach**
50g **parsley**
200g **mineral water**
2.6g **agar-agar**
7g **gelatine leaves**

1 kg **mussels in shells, cleaned**
50g **roughly chopped shallots**
1 **sprig thyme**
300g **dry white wine**

240g **dill**
180g **grapeseed oil**

15g **cornflour (cornstarch)**
90g **milk**
500g **buttermilk**
75g **horseradish, grated**
lemon juice
salt

salt flakes

Photograph page 213

Razor clams and parsley gel
Use a small spatula or rounded-off knife to release the razor clam from its shell by carefully cutting through the muscles that hold it together. Trim off everything but the long central part of the clam, freeze for 24 hours to tenderize it, then defrost. Wash and blanch the baby spinach and parsley separately in salted water. Cool in ice water when tender. Blend with the mineral water for 1½ minutes at full speed. Push through a fine sieve (strainer) into a pan and whisk in the agar-agar. Bloom the gelatine leaves in ice water while you bring the spinach and parsley mixture to the boil. Keep stirring, and take it off the heat when cooked through. When it has cooled for a minute or so add the gelatine and pour the mixture on to a flat tray in a thin, 2-mm-thick layer to set. Place in the refrigerator for 30 minutes. Place each defrosted razor clam on the gel and roll it carefully around the gel twice. Trim the sides off.

Mussel juice
Put the mussels, then the shallots, thyme and finally the white wine into a large warm pan and cook, covered, for 45 minutes. Strain, reduce to half, cool and freeze. When frozen, leave the juice to defrost on a fine cloth set over a bowl in order to clarify it. This will take 12–24 hours in the refrigerator depending on quantity.

Dill oil
Pick the dill off the stems and blanch the leaves for 5 minutes in salted water. Cool in ice water and dry completely on paper. Add the oil and process in a Thermomix at 80°C (180°F). Leave to infuse for 24 hours, then strain.

Horseradish snow
Mix the cornflour with the milk, boil the mixture in a pan, stirring it until it becomes thick and smooth, then mix with the buttermilk and the horseradish. Leave to infuse for 12 hours. Strain off and discard the horseradish and season the liquid to taste with lemon juice and salt. Freeze in Paco containers. When frozen, spin the snow for 10–15 seconds in the Pacojet. A snow-like texture will be created on the surface of the horseradish mixture. Scrape it off and repeat the procedure until you have enough for 8–10 tablespoons. Keep in the freezer.

Serving
Place a rolled razor clam in the middle of a cold soup plate, add 2 tablespoons of snow and sprinkle both with flakes of salt. Mix the ice-cold mussel juice with the dill oil in the ratio of 10:1 and pour it next to the clam. Drop flakes of salt over the clam and the snow.

HARE, WOOD AND BEECH NUTS

5–6 **fresh green walnuts**
250g **water**
115g **sugar**
70g **apple balsamic vinegar**

5 **bunches thyme (to make** 42g **when blanched)**
small **bunch parsley (to make** 12g **when blanched)**
55g **grapeseed oil**

750g **button (white) mushrooms**
½ **onion**
½ **leek**
½ **carrot**
butter, for sautéing
750g **light chicken stock**
2.25kg **water**
reduced birch wine
6 **egg whites**
20g **applewood chips**

16 **beech nuts**
4 **wet walnuts**
a little **lemon juice**
8 **chestnuts**
grapeseed oil, for frying
20 **leaves wood sorrel**
16 **sprigs heather**

2 **hare loins**
oil, for frying
15g **butter**
25g **chicken glace**

Photograph page 214

Pickled walnuts
Poke 10–12 holes in each walnut and cover with water in a bowl. Leave for 14 days, changing the water daily. Boil the nuts in fresh water until tender, cool and strain. Bring the remaining ingredients to the boil in a large pan. Add the nuts, making sure they are covered by the pickle, and when cool vacuum-pack them in bags. Leave in the refrigerator for 6–8 weeks before using.

Thyme oil
Blanch the thyme on its stems for 4–5 minutes until very tender. Cool in ice water and pull off the stems. Strain to obtain all the leaves and squeeze through a Superbag to remove the remaining water. Keep dry on kitchen paper (paper towels). Pick the leaves from the parsley stems and blanch the leaves tender. Dry as for the thyme. Process the herbs and oil in a Thermomix at full speed at 60°C (140°F) for 12 minutes. Cool and macerate for 24 hours. Strain through a fine cloth, applying pressure for a few hours, and keep in a small squeezy bottle.

Sauce
Roughly chop all the vegetables. Sauté in butter in small batches, place in a large pan with the stock, water and wine and boil for 1 hour. Strain, reduce to half and cool. Whisk the egg whites a little, add to the bouillon and heat slowly to clarify. Pass through a cloth and reduce to a sauce consistency. Toast the wood chips in a pan to release their aroma and pour the bouillon over them. Infuse for 5–8 minutes and strain.

Garnish
Crack the beech nuts and walnuts and remove the inner brown skin. Store in cold water with a few drops of lemon juice until serving. Carefully shell the chestnuts and peel off the hairy skin. Using a truffle slicer, cut half of them into 2-mm slices directly into water and discard the trimmings. Dry the slices and fry until crisp in grapeseed oil at 160°C (325°F). Grate the rest of the walnuts on a microplane. Pick the leaves of the wood sorrel and heather into ice water and spin them dry. Keep dry and cool until serving.

Hare
Trim the sinews from the loins and store in the refrigerator until about 15 minutes before serving. Sauté the loins on all sides in a little oil in a hot pan and turn down the heat. Add the butter and baste the meat for a few minutes. Pour off the fat and add the glace to glaze the meat. Rest for a few minutes before serving.

Serving
Warm the plates. Halve each loin into 2 to make 4 portions. Place a portion in the centre of each plate and arrange all the garnishes on top. Quarter half of the pickled walnuts and cut the rest in half. Add a half and 4–5 quarters to each plate. Heat the sauce and add.

LINGONBERRIES
AND
HAY CREAM

2 sheets gelatine
110g **water**
20g **trimoline**
55g **sugar**
550g **lingonberry purée**

2 **eggs**
125g **sugar**
15g **grapeseed oil**
10g **hazelnut oil**
170g **almond flour**
25g **plain (all-purpose) flour**
10g **baking powder**
270g **carrots, grated**
butter, for frying

50g **hay**
125g **cream**
200g **milk**

25g **mustard oil**

Photograph page 215

Lingonberry sorbet
Bloom the gelatine and heat the water with the trimoline and sugar. Melt the gelatine in the warm mix and add it to the purée. Freeze in Paco containers. Spin the ice in a Pacojet and then put it in a piping (pastry) bag. Squeeze out a long pipe of sorbet, cut it into 3-cm-long pieces and freeze again.

Carrot cake crumble
Preheat the oven to 160°C (325°F) and grease a 20cm diameter shallow cake tin. Beat together the eggs, sugar and oil. Sift the flours and baking powder into the egg mixture and finally add the grated carrots. Bake for 25 minutes. Cool the cake on a rack, and when cold process it to a coarse powder. Put a piece of butter in a sauté pan and fry the carrot cake crumble until golden and crisp. Cool on grease-absorbent paper.

Hay cream
Preheat the oven to 160°C (325°F) and bake the hay in it for 60 minutes. When cool, place in vacuum bags for 2–3 hours with 75g of the cream. Strain the cream off and add the milk. Pour into a siphon bottle and add 2 cartridges. Stir the contents of the bottle and keep cool until serving.

Serving
Put the plates in the freezer to get very cold. Take the sorbet from the freezer a few minutes before serving and toss it in the carrot cake crumble to cover completely. Put 7–8 pieces on each frozen plate. Shake the siphon bottle, dispense a few dots of hay cream on the plate and finish with a few drops of mustard oil.

POTATOES
LOVAGE
AND
WHEY

250g **Nadine potatoes**
250g **water**
50g **butter**
salt

20 **small potatoes**
500g **grapeseed oil**
salt, coarse and fine
125g **water**
200g **butter**
a few sprigs lovage

200g **yoghurt**
20g **butter**
180g **lovage**
60g **grapeseed oil**

12 **dill leaves**
12 **goosefoot leaves**
8 **lemon balm leaves**
8 **sprigs chervil**

4 **round slices of Västerbotten Prästost 2 mm thick and 13 cm diameter**

Photograph page 216

Potato purée

Cut up 75g of the potatoes, bring to the boil in the water and let them simmer for 2 – 3 hours to obtain a potato stock. Peel the remaining potatoes, vacuum-pack them without water and poach them in a water bath at 70°C (160°F) for 40 minutes. Warm approximately 100g of the potato stock with the butter and add the cooked potatoes. Mix, and pass through a fine sieve (strainer). Season with salt and keep warm until serving.

Potatoes and shells

Preheat the oven to 160°C (325°F). Bake half of the small potatoes for 35 minutes, then cool. Cut them in half and scoop out the insides with a parisienne cutter. Freeze the potatoes for 2 days to dry them out. Ensure the potatoes have defrosted and then carefully deep-fry them in the grapeseed oil at 160°C (325°F) until crisp, and sprinkle with fine salt. Scrub the remaining potatoes with coarse salt to remove impurities from the skins. Heat the water, cut the butter into pieces and whisk it into the water to form an emulsion. Add the lovage to the emulsion.

Sauce and oil

Pour the yoghurt into a clean cloth and let it hang over a bowl for 24 hours so that all the whey is strained off. Gently warm the whey, cut the butter into dice and add them. Pick the lovage leaves off the stems and blanch for 5 minutes in salted water. Cool on ice and dry completely on absorbent paper. Add the oil to the lovage leaves and process in a Thermomix at 80°C (180°F). Leave the oil to infuse for 24 hours and then strain.

Garnish

Pick the dill, goosefoot and lemon balm leaves from their stems and rinse in ice water. Spin them dry and place them on absorbent paper. Remove the leaves from the chervil and keep them for another dish. Rinse the chervil stems as the other herbs.

Serving

Cook the scrubbed potatoes in the butter emulsion until tender. Place a few tablespoons of the warm potato purée in the middle of a plate. Melt the cheese over the purée with a blowtorch and season with salt. Place the cooked potatoes and the fried shells next to the purée. Arrange the herbs around the plate. Add the lovage oil to the sauce, pour the mixture around the purée and serve.

BREAD,
BUTTER
AND
FAT

170g **water**
27g **wheat flour from Bornholm**
15g **rye flour**
15g **stoneground wholemeal (whole wheat) flour**

5g **yeast**
650g **water**
50g **sourdough starter**
22g **salt**
600g **wheat flour from Bornholm**
200g **wheat flour from Ölands**

125g **Swedish goat's butter**

600g **pork rind**
180g **smoked pork fat**
½ **clove garlic, chopped**
40g **unfiltered apple aquavit**
12g **salt**
1 **onion, chopped**
milk, for blanching the onion
50g **plain (all-purpose) flour**
grapeseed oil, for frying
1 **potato**

Photograph page 218

Sourdough starter

Mix all the ingredients in a large bowl and leave in a dry place at room temperature to ferment for 7 days, mixing it once every day. Twenty-four hours before using it to make bread, the sourdough starter must be fed with fresh flour and water by adding 70g of the pre-fermented sourdough to a new batch of the quantities of flour and water given in the recipe.

Bread

Dissolve the yeast in the water and add the sourdough starter and salt. Add the flours and process at low speed in a stand mixer for 5–7 minutes. Let the dough rest for 24 hours in the refrigerator. Divide into 250-g portions and shape into rounds. Preheat the oven to 235°C (455°F). Let the loaves prove (rise) at room temperature in baskets for 30 minutes, then grease a baking tray and bake them for 35 minutes.

Butter

Leave the butter at room temperature for a few hours to soften, then roll it in a piece of baking (parchment) paper to make a perfectly round 7cm diameter cylinder. Cool in the refrigerator and cut into slices 6mm thick. Make sure the butter is served just below room temperature.

Fat

Take the pork rind and fat from the refrigerator and, while still cold, put them through a meat grinder, then carefully melt them in a large pan. Keep heating, stirring from time to time, until the temperature reaches 130°C (265°F). Strain off the pork crackling and cool the melted fat. Add the garlic and aquavit, and when the fat has cooled to a thick but stirrable consistency season with salt. Blanch the onions in milk for 1 minute. Strain and cool. Dust them with the flour and fry in grapeseed oil at 180°C (350°F) until crisp and golden. Slice the potato thinly, fry the slices in the same oil until crisp, cool, then crush into small pieces. Mix together equal quantities of onions, potatoes and pork crackling. When the fat is cold spread it on to dishes and sprinkle the crispy mixture on top.

At Noma, Bread, Butter and Fat is served at the beginning of the meal to accompany the rest of the dishes.

SEA URCHINS
AND
FROZEN MILK,
CUCUMBER
AND
DILL

2–4 **sea urchins**

1 **cucumber**
20g **dill oil**

500g **water**
200g **dill**
40g **apple balsamic vinegar**
salt
1g **xanthan gum**

500g **milk**
500g **cream**

1 **small bunch dill**

Photograph page 219

Sea urchins
Wearing gloves, use strong scissors to cut carefully into the bottom of each sea urchin and work towards the sides. Cut all the way around the shell, taking care not to prick your fingers on the sharp spines, and remove the bottom. Rinse the insides of the sea urchins with cold water and remove the edible orange 'tongues' with a small teaspoon. Clean off any impurities and store the 'tongues' in the refrigerator.

Cucumber
Peel the cucumber and place the peel under a hot grill (broiler) until completely carbonized. Pass it through a fine cloth to make a powder. Use a parisienne cutter to make small balls of about 10mm diameter from the cucumber flesh. Season 7 balls per person with a little of the dill oil, adding the powder to give a grilled flavour.

Dill granita
Process the water, dill and vinegar in a Thermomix for 2 minutes at full speed. Drain the liquid and season with salt. Add the xanthan gum to a small amount of the liquid, and blend with a hand blender in a tall container. Pour the thickened mix into the main batch and freeze in a flat container in the blast freezer. Scrape with a fork and keep frozen.

Frozen milk
Mix the milk and cream, and use a hand blender to froth the mixture until a foam is created on top. Spoon it into liquid nitrogen and let freeze for 5 seconds. Turn and repeat on the other side, crushing the cloud into smaller pieces to give the consistency of a coarse granita. Keep in the freezer.

Garnish
Pick about 30 leaves off the dill stalks and soak in ice water. Pat dry and keep cold.

Serving
Place a spoon in the freezer. Put a ring cutter of approximately 130mm diameter in the middle of each diner's plate, and place 5 of the sea urchin tongues and then 7 balls of cucumber within it. With the frozen spoon, drizzle a few tablespoons of the dill granita and the frozen milk to cover the remaining area inside the ring cutter, then carefully remove it. It is important not to cover the sea urchins and cucumber. Finally add the dill.

CHICKEN SKIN AND RYEBREAD, SMOKED CHEESE AND LUMPFISH ROE

8 complete chicken skins

1 rye loaf, approximately 600g
butter

100g fresh lumpfish roe
30g smoked cheese
10g full fat (whole) milk
10g cream
5g picked dill
1g salt

Photograph page 220

Chicken skin
Preheat the oven to 160°C (325°F). Scrape the chicken skins free of fat and meat, then spread out on baking (parchment) paper, putting 2 on top of each other to create a double layer. Bake on trays, placing oven-proof weights on top, for 2 hours. When cool, cut the chicken skins into 3×10-cm pieces.

Rye bread
Preheat the oven to 160°C (325°F). Cut the loaf lengthways into 2-mm slices (a meat slicer is helpful). Cut these into pieces 4×10cm and spread out on baking trays lined with baking paper. Spray plenty of butter on top and cover with another sheet of baking paper. Put another tray on top and bake, placing ovenproof weights on top, for 18 minutes. Trim the bread pieces to 3×10cm.

Lumpfish roe
Remove any sinews from the roe by rinsing it several times while mixing it with a whisk. Strain it through a cloth for a few hours to remove excess liquid. Mix the cheese with the milk and cream and fold into the roe. Chop the dill and add to the mixture. Season with salt and store in a piping (pastry) bag.

Serving
Pipe approximately 3g of roe mixture on to a crisp ryebread. Put a piece of baked chicken skin on top, and trim off any bread or skin that sticks out. Serve with the ryebread facing up.

SMOKED QUAIL EGGS

10 **quail eggs**
20g **hay**
50g **birchwood chips**

200g **water**
100g **rose hip vinegar**

hay, to serve

Photograph page 221

Eggs
Blanch the eggs for 1 minute 30 seconds and cool them in ice water. Blanch them again for 50 seconds, cool and peel them. Take care not to break them – eggs cooked for such a short time are very soft and fragile. Finally, smoke the eggs for around 20 minutes on a slotted gastro tray in a smoker by heating it slowly with the hay and chips.

Pickle
Mix the water and vinegar, and pickle the eggs in this mixture in a vacuum-pack bag for 10 minutes. Keep warm until you are ready to serve.

Serving
Cut the hay into short lengths and use it to fill the base of an oval serving dish. Make a small incision in the bottom of each egg and lay them on the hay. With a hand held food smoker burn hay into the serving dish and cover quickly, trapping the smoke in the dish.

STEAMED EGG WHITE
AND
BIRCH WINE, WILD MUSHROOMS

8 organic eggs, each weighing approximately 55–65g

60g **white wine**
200g **wild mushroom trimmings**
butter, for sautéing
60g **ceps (fresh porcini)**
1 **shallot**
salt

200g **cep (fresh porcini) trimmings**
115g **grapeseed oil**

750g **wild mushrooms or button (white) mushrooms**
½ **onion**
½ **leek**
½ **carrot**
butter, for sautéing
750g **light chicken stock**
2.25kg **water**
6 **egg whites**
reduced birch wine

125g **wild mushrooms**
(make sure they are a variety that can be eaten raw)
1 **truffle from Gotland**

Photograph page 223

Steamed egg whites
Crack the eggs and separate the whites from the yolks. Line a plastic container with clingfilm (plastic wrap), pour in the egg whites and close with a lid. Steam at 100°C (210°F) for 45 minutes, then cool. Cut into cubes of 2.5×2.5cm and smoke for 15 minutes in the smoker.

Sautéed mushrooms and cep compote
Reduce the white wine by half. Wash the wild mushroom trimmings and cut them into small pieces. Sauté quickly and put them aside. Sauté the ceps in plenty of butter until caramelized. Chop the shallots and sauté until soft. Put the ceps and shallots into a blender and process in a few short bursts. Season with salt and the reduced white wine.

Cep oil
Preheat the oven to 80°C (180°F). Place the trimmings in a metal container and pour the oil over them. Cover the container tightly with clingfilm and cook it in the oven for 12 hours. Strain through a cloth, pour into a small squeezy bottle and keep refrigerated.

Mushroom bouillon
Roughly chop all the vegetables. Sauté everything in small batches, then combine the vegetables with the stock and water and boil for 1 hour. Strain the bouillon, reduce it to half and cool. Whisk the egg whites a little, add to the bouillon and heat it gently to clarify. Strain the bouillon through a cloth and season with reduced birch wine.

Garnish
Clean the mushrooms, keep a few whole and cut the rest into small pieces. Slice the whole ones finely on a mandolin. Brush the truffle to clean it, and slice finely.

Serving
Warm up the smoked egg whites and place them in the middle of a bowl. Surround with tablespoons of the cep compote and the sautéed mushroom trimmings. Drizzle the cep oil over the egg whites and garnish with the raw mushroom and truffle slices. Pour the bouillon into a jug (pitcher) to serve at the table.

OXTAIL
AND
DARK BEER, APPLE
AND
JERUSALEM ARTICHOKE

2.5kg **oxtail, cut in pieces**
oil, for rubbing
salt
250g **red wine**
1.25kg **light chicken stock**
125g **dark lager**
1 **onion**
1 **carrot**
1 **leek**
20g **shallots**
1 **sprig thyme**
¼ **lemon**
butter, for sautéing
small bunch thyme

100g **reduced oxtail stock**
35g **brown butter**
5g **verbena leaves**

5g **Gellan**
500g **organic apple juice**

2 sprigs **verbena, mainly small leaves**
500g **large Jerusalem artichokes**

50g **balsamic apple vinegar**
a little butter
1 large **Mutzu apple or 2 smaller ones**

Photograph page 224

Oxtail
Preheat the oven to 225°C (440°F). Rub the oxtail pieces in oil and salt. Brown the meat in a roasting tin in the oven, turning from time to time to brown evenly. Peel and dice the vegetables. Reduce the oven heat to 80°C (180°F). Combine the meat with the wine, stock, beer and vegetables in a deep gastro tray. Add water to cover, and cover with clingfilm (plastic wrap). Put a lid on top and add another layer of clingfilm. Cook the meat in the oven for 6–8 hours. Pick the meat off the bones and place in a mixing bowl. Strain the cooking liquid and reduce. Chop the shallots and the smaller amount of thyme, add the zest of the lemon and sauté briefly in a little butter. When the oxtail liquid has reduced to a glace-like consistency add 2 tablespoons of it to the meat together with the sautéed shallots, thyme and lemon zest, and the bunch of thyme and mix thoroughly.

Sauce
Heat the reduced oxtail stock and the brown butter in a pan. Add the verbena, cover with clingfilm, and infuse for 20 minutes. Strain the sauce.

Gel
Whisk the Gellan into the cold juice and pour into a pan. Bring the juice to the boil, whisking constantly, and let it cook for 60 seconds. Pour into white trays to a depth of 2mm and cool. Cut into 12-cm squares and store in layers on baking (parchment) paper.

Garnish
Pick all the small leaves from the verbena, wash in ice water, dry and keep in the refrigerator. Cut the artichokes into 1-cm slices, then into rounds with a 2.5–3-cm cutter. Blanch the artichokes in salted water for 2–3 minutes and cool in ice water.

Serving
Heat the oxtail in a small pan or in a plastic container in the microwave and place a 50-g portion on each person's plate. Heat the gel squares, brush the tops with vinegar and cover the meat with gel. Heat the artichokes in a tablespoon of butter. Slice the apple thinly on a mandolin and then cut into 4-cm rounds. Overlap the artichokes and apples on top of the gel. Sprinkle verbena leaves all over and drizzle sauce around the plate.

TRUFFLE DESSERT

80g **double (heavy) or whipping cream**
55g **egg whites**
30g **sugar**
3 **sheets gelatine**
250g **quark**
2g **hay ash**

15g **sugar**
100g **egg whites**
100g **truffle trimmings**

35g **sugar**
125g **water**
260g **mineral water**
7g **glucose**
60g **truffle trimmings**
2g **truffle oil**
4g **lemon juice**
0.6g **citric acid**
20g **fresh truffle**
4g **squid ink**
3 **leaves gelatine**

60g **dark beer**
12g **egg white powder**
45g **icing (confectioners') sugar**
5g **cornflour (cornstarch)**
35g **tipo '00' flour**

2.5g **egg white powder**
50g **egg whites**
80g **sugar**
25g **water**
5g **apple balsamic vinegar**

Photograph page 229

Truffle/quark mousse

Whip the cream to soft peaks. In a separate bowl, whisk the egg whites with the sugar to a meringue. Bloom the gelatine and add to a small amount of the quark. Heat until the gelatine is dissolved and add the ash. Add the heated quark to the rest of the quark and fold the whipped cream and then the meringue into the mixture to create a mousse. Put in plastic containers in the refrigerator to set.

Truffle meringue flakes

Preheat the oven to 90°C (195°F). Whisk the sugar and egg whites to a meringue and fold the truffle trimmings into it. Spread the mixture on a silpat and dry in the oven for 4 hours. Crush the cooked meringue into flakes.

Truffle granita

Bring the sugar and water to the boil and let cool. Mix in all the other ingredients except the gelatine and process in a Thermomix for 2 minutes. Bloom the gelatine and add it to the previously heated mixture, then put in the freezer and scrape with a fork once set.

Branches

Whisk the beer and egg white powder together until they start to foam. Sift the icing sugar into the mix, stir together and add the flours. Rest the dough for 2 hours, then pat into a piping (pastry) bag. Preheat the oven to 160°C (325°F). Pipe the mixture on to silpats in small branch shapes and bake for 6–7 minutes.

Burnt meringues

Place the egg white powder and egg whites in the bowl of a stand mixer. Combine the sugar, water and vinegar in a pan and heat until it forms a caramel at 121°C (250°F). During this time, once the caramel has reached 110°C (230°F), start whisking the egg mixture. When the caramel reaches 121°C (250°F), reduce the whisking speed, and slowly pour the caramel into the bowl to make an Italian meringue. Make sure it is whisked through, then place it in a bath of liquid nitrogen.

Serving

Break the meringue into small rough pieces directly on to the plate in an irregular pattern and burn with a blowtorch until golden. Place 2 tablespoons of mousse per person on top of the meringue pieces, coating them completely, then mould them with your hands into a truffle shape. Sprinkle the granita and the meringue flakes on top and add 3–4 branches per plate.

KING CRAB
AND
LEEKS IN ASHES

2 king crab claws

1kg **bag of hay**

1kg **mussels**
½ **shallot, roughly chopped**
1 **sprig thyme**
300g **dry white wine, plus a little extra to taste**
50g **cream**
10g **butter**
salt and pepper
reduced white wine

8 **large leeks**
60g **water**

50g **breadcrumbs**
10g **butter**
salt

50g **butter, plus extra for frying**
85g **water**
salt

Photograph page 230

King crab
Use small strong scissors to cut open the shell, then carefully pull out the meat. Roll the meat up firmly in clingfilm (plastic wrap) in a cylindrical shape.

Burnt hay
Set fire to the hay in a big fireproof container and let it burn for 2–3 hours. Make sure that there are no solid lumps left, and when it is completely cool pass it through a fine cloth or sieve (strainer).

Mussel sauce
Put the mussels, then the shallot, thyme and lastly the white wine into a warm pan and cook, covered on the stove top for 45 minutes. In a separate pan heat the cream and reduce it to one-third. Strain the mussels, reserve the liquid and reduce by half, then add the butter and reduced cream. Season, and add more reduced wine to increase the acidity if necessary.

Leeks
Cut the green tops from the leeks and use for another dish. Boil the white parts for 8–9 minutes in salted water, then cool in ice water. Peel off 3–4 layers to leave only the extra-sweet part of each leek and trim into 10-cm lengths.

Fried breadcrumbs
Melt the butter in a sauté pan, add the breadcrumbs, fry until golden and crisp, then season with salt.

Serving
Poach the king crab rolls at 58°C (135°F) for 4 minutes, pull them out of the clingfilm, then roll them slowly in a pan with warm butter and season with salt. Heat the water and whisk in the 50g of butter to make an emulsion. Add the leeks and warm them through. Peel off the outside layer and roll the leeks in the burnt hay. Tap off excess ash and trim the king crab roll to the same size as the leeks. Heat the mussel sauce in a pan, adjust the seasoning and acidity and foam up the sauce with an immersion blender. Put the king crab and leeks next to each other on the plate in the shape of a square, and serve the sauce and breadcrumbs separately at the table.

REINDEER
WITH
CELERIAC
AND
WILD HERB GEL

200g **trimmed reindeer shoulder**
600g **trimmed reindeer loin**
175g **cream**
salt

300g **hay**
2 **celeriac (celery root)**
500g **salt**
500g **plain (all-purpose) flour**
300g **water**
1 **Granny Smith apple**

50g **tarragon**
25g **wild chervil**
15g **ground elder**
150g **mineral water**
8g **wild fennel seeds**
2g **Gellan**
50g **piece raw liquorice**

150g **reduced chicken glace**
30g **brown butter**
apple balsamic vinegar
1 **tablespoon chopped shallots**
1 **teaspoon chopped parsley**
1 **teaspoon ramsons (wild garlic) capers**

chicken glace
butter

Photograph page 231

Reindeer

Vacuum-pack the shoulder and cook at 85°C (185°F) for 6 hours. Pick the meat out in strips and chop roughly. Trim the loin and cut it in long strips of about 80g per portion. Combine the surplus meat with the cream and blend very quickly. Pass this mousse through a fine sieve (strainer), add the shoulder meat, fold together and season with salt. Pipe this mixture on to the loin strips with a piping (pastry) bag. Roll the loin strips in clingfilm (plastic wrap) and poach for 14 minutes at 70°C (160°). Each roll will serve 2 people.

Garnish

Preheat the oven to 220°C (425°F). Burn the hay until reduced to ashes. Peel one celeriac and roll it in the hay. Mix the salt, flour and water into a dough and roll it out to cover the celeriac, leaving the bottom uncovered. Cook in the oven for 20 minutes, then reduce the heat to 160°C (325°F) to finish cooking for another 35–45 minutes depending on the size. When cold, slice the celeriac and then cut further to 2cm diameter rounds. Allow 3–4 pieces per portion. Finely slice the second (raw) celeriac on a meat slicer and trim the slices to 5cm diameter rounds. Finely slice the apple and trim to the same size.

Wild herb gel

Blanch the tarragon, chervil and ground elder until tender, cool, then blend with the mineral water and wild fennel seeds. Strain through a cloth and mix with the Gellan. Boil for 2 seconds, pour on to a flat tray and cool. Cut out in the same way as the baked celeriac and grate the liquorice on top.

Brown butter sauce

Gently heat the glace and the brown butter, taste and add extra vinegar to increase the acidity if necessary. Add the remaining ingredients just before serving.

Serving

Sauté the meat on all sides, glaze it in the chicken glace and cut into 2 round pieces per portion. Heat the cooked celeriac in a little butter and dust with the burnt hay. Lightly warm the herb gels on a hot surface. Arrange meat and celeriac rounds on a plate, then add the raw celeriac, raw apple and gels. Pour some brown butter sauce on to the plate and serve.

FINGERLING POTATOES
AND
SPECK

250g **yoghurt**
30g **butter**

125g **smoked speck fat**

625g **fingerling potatoes**
150g **full fat (whole) milk**
150g **cream**
65g **butter**

25g **truffles from Gotland**
3g **chicken glace**
5g **light chicken stock**
24g **truffle oil**
15g **grapeseed oil**
apple balsamic vinegar
salt

Photograph page 232

Whey sauce

Pour the yoghurt on to a cloth and hang over a bowl for 24 hours to strain off the whey. The yield of whey will be approximately half the amount of yoghurt. Heat the whey slightly and add the butter in pieces.

Smoked fat

Boil the fat in unsalted water in a large pan for 2 hours. Cool, keeping it under pressure between trays. Freeze the fat, then slice it finely on a meat slicer. Cut out into 13-cm discs.

Potato purée

Boil the potatoes until tender. Strain off the liquid and leave the potatoes in the uncovered pan for a few seconds to release some steam. Heat the milk, cream and butter in a small pan. Pass the potatoes through a drum sieve (strainer) into a large bowl and combine with the milk mixture. Mix together gently and pass through a fine sieve. Keep warm until serving.

Truffle purée

Peel the truffles and blend with the chicken glace and stock. Emulsify the oils in this mixture as though making a mayonnaise. Season to taste with apple balsamic vinegar and salt.

Serving

Heat the potato purée in a small pan and place a small amount in the centre of a plate. Top with a small, round tablespoon of truffle purée. Heat the sheet of smoked fat on a hot surface and cover the purée with it. Heat the whey sauce, froth with an immersion blender and drizzle around the plate.

JERUSALEM ARTICHOKES AND TOASTED HAY OIL, YOGHURT AND TRUFFLES

800g **Jerusalem artichokes**
60g **brown butter**
200g **light chicken stock**

125g **hazelnuts**

2 **large truffles from Gotland plus** 40g **truffles of any size**
white wine vinegar
salt

45g **full-fat yoghurt**

25g **hay**
200g **grapeseed oil**
salt

Photograph page 235

Jerusalem artichokes
Wash the artichokes thoroughly. Vacuum-pack half of them with the brown butter and the remaining half with the chicken stock. Steam the first mixture at 90°C (195°F) for 40–42 minutes, depending on the size of the artichokes and cool in ice water. Steam the second mixture at 80°C (180°F) for 12 hours and then strain the liquid. Reduce the liquid to half, to use later for diluting the truffle purée. Cut the artichokes cooked in butter into 1-cm-thick slices and trim them to approximately 1cm diameter. Prepare about 15 pieces per person.

Hazelnut purée
Preheat the oven to 160°C (325°F). Toast the nuts on a tray in the oven for 20 minutes. While still warm, blend to a fine purée.

Truffle slices and truffle sauce
finely slice the big truffles and punch out 10 pieces per person in different sizes. Peel the remaining truffles and combine them, along with the trimmings from the large truffles, with the reduced Jerusalem artichoke liquid. Bring to the boil, blend to a smooth sauce and season with white wine vinegar and salt.

Yoghurt
Pour the yoghurt on to a cloth and let it hang over a bowl for 15 minutes so excess whey can drain off, then transfer the yoghurt to a squeezy bottle.

Hay oil
Preheat the oven to 200°C (400°F). Toast the hay in the oven for 1 hour then, while still warm, combine it with the oil and a pinch of salt, and vacuum-pack everything together. Leave to macerate for 24 hours.

Serving
Warm the artichoke and brown butter mixture, and drain. Sprinkle with salt and cover 4–5 of the artichoke slices with the hazelnut purée. Arrange all the artichoke slices on a plate and cover with truffle slices. Add a few dots of yoghurt, pour the warm sauce around the other components and finally drizzle hay oil around the plate.

CREAMY BARLEY AND GRAINS, WHEATGRASS AND TRUFFLE

10g **whole oats**
10g **whole barley grains**
10g **whole einkorn wheat grains**
10g **whole kamut grains**
10g **whole emmer grains**
10g **whole spelt grains**
10g **whole buckwheat**
15g **Västerbotten cheese, grated**

100g **water**
1g **dried woodruff**
1g **dried verbena**
1g **dried thuja pine cones**
1g **dried camomile**
15g **ground millet**
2g **milk**

100g **truffles from Gotland**
12g **chicken glace**
20g **light chicken stock**
24g **truffle oil**
60g **grapeseed oil**
apple balsamic vinegar
salt

1.25 kg **pork ribs cut into small pieces**
½ **onion**
½ **apple**
1 **stick celery**
2 **sprigs thyme**

40g **wheatgrass**
150g **water**
roast pork juice
apple balsamic vinegar

10g **flax seeds**
10g **pumpkin seeds**

Photograph page 238

Corn stew

Rinse all the ingredients in water except the Västerbotten cheese. Cook the oats for 10 minutes in lightly salted water. Cook the barley and einkorn for 15 minutes. Cook the kamut, emmer and spelt for 20 minutes. Rinse them all in cold water until cool, and keep dry until serving. Soak the buckwheat in plenty of cold water for 24 hours and strain off the excess liquid.

Millet porridge

Bring the water to the boil and add the dried herbs. Leave to infuse for 5 minutes, then strain. Discard the herbs. Mix the herb tea with the millet and milk and cook in a pan for 8–10 minutes, stirring, until tender and creamy. Pass through a fine sieve (strainer).

Truffle disc

Peel the truffles and blend with the chicken glace and stock. Emulsify the oils in the smooth mixture as with a mayonnaise. Season with vinegar and salt to taste. Spread the purée in a fine layer on small sheets of baking (parchment) paper, approximately 10g of purée per sheet. Freeze the purée, then cut out in rounds of 8cm diameter. Keep in the freezer until serving.

Roast pork juice

Preheat the oven to 230°C (450°F). Roast the ribs for 30 minutes until very golden. Peel the vegetables and pan-roast them. Lower the oven temperature to 80°C (180°F). Combine all the ingredients in a deep gastro and add water to cover. Place a lid on the gastro and cook in the oven for 10 hours. Strain the liquid and reduce by half.

Wheatgrass juice

Chop the wheatgrass roughly and blend it with the water. Put through a fine sieve and season with a little of the roast pork juice and vinegar.

Serving

Mix all the cooked grains with the millet porridge and the cheese, and heat through. Add the pumpkin and flax seeds and season with salt. Place in the middle of a plate and cover with a frozen truffle disc. Heat the truffle disc with a blowtorch, warm the wheatgrass juice and pour it around the dish.

MILK SKIN
AND
SALSIFY,
RAPESEED
AND
TRUFFLE PURÉE

100g **truffles from Gotland**
12g **chicken glace**
20g **light chicken stock**
24g **truffle oil**
60g **grapeseed oil**
apple balsamic vinegar
salt

1000g **milk**
50g **cream**
30g **milk protein**

8 **large stems of salsify**

2 **slices white bread**
25g **rapeseed (canola) oil**

apple balsamic vinegar
wild herbs
salt

Photograph page 240

Truffle purée

Peel the truffles and blend with the chicken glace and stock, then emulsify the truffle and grapeseed oils in the smooth mixture as for mayonnaise. Season with vinegar and salt.

Milk skin

Mix all the ingredients and heat in a pan to around 70°C (160°F). Skim off the first few skins, which will be very fragile. When a firm skin is formed, pull it off the pan with both hands and store on baking (parchment) paper. Repeat until 4–5 perfect skins have been produced.

Salsify

Peel the salsify and cut each piece to a length of approximately 12cm, then blanch for 3–4 minutes in boiling water. Cool in ice water and pat dry, then sauté in a pan with oil until golden-brown on all sides.

Crispy bread

Pull the bread into 10–15 small, irregular pieces and sauté them in butter in a pan for 2–3 minutes until crisp and golden.

Sauce

Heat the cream, milk and rapeseed oil together in a pan.

Serving

Heat the milk skin on a hot surface or by putting it in a hot oven for 2 minutes. Take a warm plate for each serving, smear a spoonful of truffle purée across the surface and place two pieces of salsify next to it. Add a few drops of vinegar, cover with the milk skin, and pour a spoonful of sauce on top. Place a selection of wild herbs, salt and the crispy bread on top of the milk skin.

OVER-RIPE PEARS
AND
MALT OIL, SKYR
AND
WILD CHERVIL

55g **trimoline**
60g **water**
145g **whole milk**
1g **stabilizer**
1g **maltodextrin**
1.5g **gelatine**
375g **skyr**
1g **lemon juice**
1g **salt**

75g **powdered malt**
200g **grapeseed oil**

1.2 kg **Doyenne du Comice pears**
2g **citric acid**
100g **acidic pear cider**

80g **sugar**
40g **water**
50g **egg whites**
2.5g **dried woodruff**

2 sprigs **wild chervil**

2 **over-ripe Doyenne du Comice pears**

Photograph page 242

Skyr ice cream

Cook the trimoline and water to a syrup, then cool. Bring a little of the milk to the boil with the stabilizer and maltodextrin. Bloom the gelatine, and add before the mixture cools. Hand blend the rest of the ingredients with the mixture, then freeze in Paco containers.

Malt oil

Mix the malt and oil and process in a Thermomix for 3–4 minutes. Keep in a squeezy bottle.

Pear sauce

Peel and core the pears and drop them into ice water. Vacuum-pack with the other ingredients and steam at 80°C (180°F) for 30 minutes. Blend and strain.

Woodruff meringue

Heat the sugar and water in a pan and lightly whisk the egg whites in a separate bowl. When the caramel has reached 121°C (250°F), whisk it into the whites to make a meringue. Fold the woodruff through the mixture and pipe very small 'kisses' on a silpat. Dry in a dehydrator at 60°C (140°F) for 4–5 hours.

Garnish

Pick the chervil into ice water and keep cold until serving.

Serving

Put the plates in the freezer to get very cold. Rub the peel off the over-ripe pears. With the tip of a teaspoon scoop 3 irregular pieces of pear flesh per person. Process the ice cream in a Pacojet and place a few tablespoons on each frozen plate. Add the pieces of over-ripe pear and the chervil leaves. Shake the squeezy bottle, split the pear sauce with the malt oil and add to the plate. Sprinkle woodruff meringues over the entire plate

THE
RAW
MATERIALS

René Redzepi

Hanne Letoft from South Zealand

In this book I describe nine of our closest collaborators and producers. Many of them are large suppliers with whom we work closely on a daily basis. However, our network stretches much further and wider. A safe estimate would be around sixty or seventy people over the whole of the Nordic region. I can best describe the majority of these people as enthusiastic hobby farmers and growers, who can supply everything from forgotten varieties of gooseberry to pine shoots, young lambs from the West Jutland marshes to walnuts from the western part of Zealand. If we were to describe them all they would fill a whole book just by themselves, and they perhaps deserve this one day – but one thing at a time.

Noma's suppliers are generally people who also have a day job, or who have recently retired, and have always had some kind of interest in and access to farming or the countryside. For example, our supplier of wild blackberries is a seasoned football coach who sets time aside each year to forage on our behalf. Our supplier of samphire from the salt marshes on the west coast of Jutland works for the local butcher, and our walnut collector is a journalist with the BBC. Another good example is the director of a major Danish media company who keeps bees and sells us delicious honey every year. He also brews the best mead I have ever tasted.

Many of these suppliers provide very few products and often in very small quantities, but enough to make a difference to Noma for a few weeks each year. When you add them all together, their combined energy and contributions are a very important factor in our cuisine and in my everyday life. The little meetings we have at about the same time every year – depending, of course, on the wind and the weather, which can advance or delay the seasons by a few weeks – are special and give me just as much pleasure as the actual changing of the seasons. It's like a shot in the arm for me, when all these people turn up one after the other with their harvest and proudly show it off to everyone in the kitchen. It's wonderful to see their delight in their produce, and you feel proud to be one of those who pass on their thoughts and ideas from the raw material to the plate.

Hanne Letoft represents the hobby farming enthusiasts. A recently retired secretary, she has always been out and about in the countryside because of her passion for horses and mushrooms – it is often mushrooms that first excite most outdoor people.

Today Hanne lives with her husband, horses and dogs near Haslev in southern Zealand, where she is surrounded by woodland. She supplies almost everything we might just happen to need. It could be wood sorrel – or it could be cowslips. She also comes up with new suggestions for raw materials and does a lot of research herself. For example, it was Hanne who introduced us to bulrushes – an unbeatable ingredient that tastes almost exactly like fresh palm marrow. Hanne is just one example. There are others like her, who have presented us with discoveries we wouldn't have made by ourselves. Hanne and all the other amateur enthusiasts have proved to be indispensable to our cuisine and its continuing development.

Photograph page 44

Søren
Brandt Wiuff
from
Lammefjorden

Søren, born in 1956, is a native of Lammefjorden, a drive of an hour or so from Copenhagen. His father was a Lammefjorden farmer and Søren himself has had an interest in agriculture ever since he first grew some tulips as a four-year-old. After studying at university in Copenhagen and travelling the world, he returned to the land. Since then he has taken over from his father, and has now extended his arable farm at Lammefjorden to 60 hectares. Søren is one of the biggest and most important suppliers of market garden produce to Danish restaurants.

All my life I have felt an attachment to the Lammefjorden region. When I was a child we went there to visit my maternal grandparents, and I remember the long walks in the cornfields, trips to Dragsholm Castle and paddling on the beaches at Tuse Næs. I remember my grandmother buying freshly dug potatoes, carrots, newly-laid eggs and lots of other good things from the Lammefjorden farmers. I also remember how irritating I felt it was to have to make these individual stops, when we could just as well have bought it all together down in the supermarket. At home in Copenhagen we didn't have a video player, and one more stop meant I would have an even longer wait to get to my grandparents' home to watch a film on their machine. Much has changed since then. My grandparents no longer live in Egemosevej, so close to the Lammefjorden area – and nowadays I really appreciate visiting the farmers!

As its name suggests, the Lammefjord was originally a stretch of water. In 1850 Baron Georg Frederik Otto Zythpen-Adeler of Dragsholm took the first steps in reclaiming this land from the sea. It was a long and arduous project, with the water level being lowered in stages, and it was only completed in 1943. The first pioneering farmers, however, had moved out along the Lammefjord as early as 1882. The land is below sea level and these early farmers just hoped that the embankment would hold when the next floods occurred. Although tests had been carried out before the draining work was started to make sure that the fjord bed was suitable to be turned into agricultural land, nobody yet knew what could be grown there. A lot of experimentation with crops was done in order to understand the soil better and to see what might grow best there, and in the end Lammefjorden has become best known for its carrots, potatoes and, to some extent, its asparagus.

Given this history of pioneer growers and crop experimentation, it almost feels as if time has stood still on Brogård, Søren Wiuff's farm. Here they are still experimenting, as in the old days, except that asparagus and carrots have been replaced by coriander and giant Bulgarian leeks. I associate Søren with innovation and the pioneering spirit. He is constantly looking for new ways of exploiting the land, and is always experimenting with new seeds and exotic plants and roots. He says that it is the excitement that drives his work – or in fact the process rather than the work. Experiencing how the vegetables grow nourishes his spirit and gives meaning to his way of life, and I believe him. His never-ending efforts to create high-quality vegetables, fruit and plants means that it could hardly be otherwise.

Søren is mainly associated with his asparagus, and, in my opinion, that's a mistake. It is juicy, sweet, full of flavour and delivered on the day it's harvested, but for me, Søren is more than the king of asparagus. He's an enthusiast who is helping to drive market gardening towards flavour and character via diversity and innovation. He is an inspiration and a friend, and is always ready to assist Noma in making further advances. He demonstrates this attitude in everything he grows: the six varieties of beetroot, the ten varieties of lettuce; the spinach, cabbages and carrots in many colours and sizes. Then there are the coriander and other newer, more modern ingredients – all of fantastic quality. The more we extend our collaboration with Søren, the easier it is to prepare great dishes. I used to travel to Lammefjorden to see my grandparents. Now I am drawn there by Søren and his wonderful crops.

Photograph page 79

Roland
Rittmann
from
Anderslöv

Roland Rittmann is one of the most persistent people I have ever met. I mean that in a purely positive way. He is also one of the most visionary and energetic people I know – though not when it comes to closing deals, but we'll come back to that later...

In just a few years, Roland's business has grown along with the attention that Noma has attracted in the big wide world outside Denmark. It is his vision that has enabled his little company to expand from a garage site to a small farm with six employees. Today he supplies wild plants to restaurants throughout Scandinavia.

Roland was born in Skåne in southern Sweden in 1947. Even as a child he was fascinated by birds, wild plants and especially mushrooms. After school he trained as a chemistry, mathematics and biology teacher. During the twenty or so years he spent working as a teacher he maintained close contact with the land. Alongside his school activities he worked as a field biologist. He was also politically active, especially in the anti-nuclear movement, and was one of the driving forces of the opposition to the Barsebäck nuclear power station in southern Sweden, which has now been shut down. Among other things he was the instigator of the 1976 Barsebäck March – the first mass demonstration against the use of nuclear power in Sweden.

Later on he developed hearing problems, and had to retire from teaching. He was offered retraining with an IT course, and had just qualified as an IT technician when the 'dot.com bubble' burst at the beginning of the new millennium. So Roland went back to roaming the countryside. After all, it was a perfectly natural step for him to take. But in fact it was his wife, Karin, whom a lot of restaurants now have to thank for the fact that Roland supplies us with such good things.

While he was unemployed, Roland had begun to collect large quantities of mushrooms and had filled up all the freezers and store rooms in their home. Eventually Karin told him he had to stop. She made him sell the mushrooms instead of having them take up much-needed space at home. So Roland took a little stall in the local market in the university city of Lund. He was soon surprised by how big a demand there was for mushrooms – especially from chefs. So he took the plunge, and in 2004 set up the company Jordnära Natur & Kultur. It was around this time that Roland and I first came across one another. I think it was at the beginning of April, so a good five months after Noma had opened. He rang to ask if ours was the restaurant that wanted to focus on Scandinavian cuisine, and if so, whether we thought our menus might involve mushrooms and wild plants from southern Sweden. I was immediately gripped by his enthusiasm and persistence and told him he should come across the bridge to Denmark to see us. Some of the people who were already supplying us with products from the wild were doing it mainly as a hobby. Suddenly here was someone who wanted to build a business around it. In those days, it was still considered quaint and old-fashioned to expend your energy on anything original and local. Everybody in Scandinavia was into tapas and wonderful hams, oils and anchovies from Spain – not ground elder and sea rocket.

During one of my first conversations with Roland, he remarked that deep down we humans are a big band of collectors. After all, *homo sapiens* had been living on roots, leaves and plants gathered from nature since the dawn of time. He said we had a 'collecting gene' inside us in the form of a natural instinct, which just needed to be reawakened. It was only a matter of time before it emerged again. He also told me that in his opinion people had become so determinedly materialistic and had grown so rich that a backlash in the direction of what was honest and original was only to be expected. He explained that our guests would probably not know what they had been missing and that it would be our job to tell them – and, of course, he could supply some of the raw materials.

Roland had many more arguments in favour of my doing business with him rather than anyone else. And to be honest, it can sometimes be difficult to escape from Roland once he gets going. Despite his great success, he's one of the worst salesmen I have ever met! Nevertheless, his sheer persistence, energy, visionary thinking and care for nature drive his business forward and always amaze me.

Photograph page 91

Roderick
Sloan
from
Bodø

Roderick is a very special person. He was born and bred in 1970 in the north of Scotland, but in the late 1990s settled in Bodø, north of the Arctic Circle in Norway. He is married to a Norwegian and has two sons. Roderick originally trained as a cook, but now works mainly as a fisherman and diver. He's one of those types who don't seem to care what clothes they wear or what car they drive. Maybe he smokes a bit too much, and he talks a bit too much as well. In fact, Roderick talks all the time when you are in his company. It may be about fresh fish, frozen fish, vegetables, exotic food, kitchen jargon, food politics, food for children and young people... It doesn't really matter. As long as the conversation involves raw materials and their production and preparation, Roderick will talk. If the conversation suddenly changes character and turns to trivialities, like a good film, he will immediately bring it back on track. Roderick often holds the floor, but in a good way. A constant stream of sensible, considered points flows from his lips, and his enormous enthusiasm shines out of everything he says.

Among other items, Roderick supplies us with sea urchins. These small, delicate creatures weigh between 100 and 120 grams and he packs them in boxes holding fifty-five each. The sea urchins are covered with cloths soaked with sea water to give them nourishment and are delivered alive a maximum of twenty-four hours after being taken from the sea. The season is relatively short and runs from November to the end of February. During this period, the sea urchins are full of roe. Roderick's Arctic sea urchins are sweeter in taste and have a slightly less intense iodine flavour than those I have sampled in other parts of the world. They have a distinct flavour of the sea, best described as something between oysters, mussels and razor clams.

'Where do sea urchins come from?' asked one of our waiters, the evening before they first appeared on the menu. Another waiter boldly replied, 'They grow on trees.' I once experienced the great efforts Roderick and his team go to in order to supply them as fresh as possible. You must be made of something special and have an indefinable passion for your work to go to these lengths. In the middle of January they start up the boat in Bodø harbour and head out into rough seas in temperatures ten degrees centigrade below freezing. They wear an extra twenty kilos of diving gear to jump into nature's ice-bath. Slowly and carefully the creatures are placed in linen sacks, whilst Roderick moves to the rhythm of the waves. With each dive he manoeuvres about under the water for up to thirty minutes, using the surge of each wave to propel him along the seabed. After that it gets too cold. The typical working day lasts ten to twelve hours. So no, sea urchins don't grow on trees.

I know that at the moment we are Roderick's only customer, and I can't thank him enough for being willing to go through all the hardship, winter after winter, that is necessary in order to supply us with a few kilos of sea urchins every week for three to four months a year. OK, sometimes he sends fresh gulls' eggs as well, but all the same... I have often wondered why he does it. It can't be for the money. I believe that Roderick enjoys the fact that people appreciate his exceptional professionalism and dedication; the fact that, somewhere out there, people are sitting in a restaurant delighting in the way we have presented the fruits of his labours. I believe that his reward is making people happy.

Photograph page 133

Chris
from
North
Zealand

'A good banker is important.' That was one of the pieces of advice I picked up along the way before Noma opened when I visited a famous Copenhagen restaurateur. 'And a lawyer. Find a good one and you'll be safely covered. Then the restaurant will run well', he predicted.

At that time I was at my wits' end because there were so many details to be sorted out. What cutlery should we use? What were we going to do about the waiters' shirts? Where would we get wild duck and walnuts for the first menu? Where should the wine cellar be located? How many employees should we start off with? Where should the waste bins be put? And so on.

There were so many decisions, big and small, waiting to be made all the time. I had never attempted opening and running a restaurant before. In fact, it came as a shock to find such a big difference between working as an employee and becoming head chef, director and co-owner with responsibility for everything. After all, I had come straight from a job as sous-chef at Kong Hans where I had a relatively free hand when it came to being creative and influencing the menu, plus a large area of responsibility for the general running of the kitchen together with Thomas Rode Andersen. I was sure that opening a restaurant couldn't be very different from what I already knew. Maybe it would require an extra ten per cent to cope with the administration, but surely not 2000 – 3000 per cent!

So the fatherly advice from a colleague in the restaurant business who had tried it all a couple of times before was to get a banker and a lawyer. A couple of years later, fate decreed that at least part of this was implemented.

Chris calls himself 'a hobby farmer'. In fact he wasn't trained to cultivate the soil, but we'll come to that later. Chris was born in England in 1950 of Danish and English parentage. He studied geography at the University of London, among other places, but moved to Denmark as a twenty-six-year-old. He now lives in North Zealand, not far from Niels Stokholm, who is also described in this book. On his four acres of land he runs an organic hobby farm together with his wife Sigrid. Like all the other producers, Chris is an incredibly positive person. In fact I would say that, despite all the hard work, the common denominator for all our suppliers, whether named in this book or not, is their friendly, warm and positive attitude. There must be a special energy in the soil.

For Chris it is important that farming should remain at the hobby level, which means that he can continue to enjoy working in agriculture purely to meet the demands of quality. He is not interested in quantity. He supplies small fennel bulbs and walnuts, among other things, but his great strengths are his herbs, salads and flowers. I don't know how he gets so much taste into his herbs and flowers. The tarragon has a deep, intense flavour, his angelica is almost overwhelming, and the salsify flowers are unique. Since summer 2004, when we first began to deal with Chris, our collaboration has deepened through mutual inspiration and respect. It also means a lot that, just as we do every day with the dishes in the kitchen, Chris takes our suggestions on board and comes up with his own ideas on how we can best work to discover and express the special characteristics of our region.

Chris has been hobby farming since the 1990s, interrupted only by a period spent in Turkey where he was working at what is still his main occupation – the banking industry. Now I just need to find a lawyer who wants to be a fisherman in his spare time...

Photograph page 157

Niels Stokholm
from
Dronningmølle

There's an unusual sort of calm about Niels Stokholm. This farmer from South Jutland always seems so gentle and well balanced, and I always feel very secure in his presence. On several occasions I have met up with Niels when I have been more pressured and stressed than usual. But after spending time with him, I have experienced some of those rare moments when the pressure makes sense, and I can begin to plan ahead with renewed energy.

Niels's whole approach to life and work feels integrated, natural and harmonious. For me, seeing him on his farm, in his true element, is like looking back in time or into a dream of people living in perfect harmony with livestock, the soil and nature. Over the years, he says, he has unconsciously become one with his farm. He thinks that, as a farmer, not only are you able to perfect your knowledge in the best possible way but also, over time, you learn from the place, the animals and the surroundings. The more deeply involved you become in your work, the better you become at noticing all the details that must be addressed in order to achieve the best possible harmonic cycle.

Niels was born in southern Denmark, close to the German border, in 1933. His family were farmers, and for his first eighteen years, he lived on the farm and took part in its everyday activities. He then trained as a civil engineer, specializing in the foundations of large buildings. After more than twenty years away from farming, he returned in his early forties. In the intervening period, agriculture had undergone sweeping changes. A more specialised, industrialized kind of farming was now the norm, which was a long way from his romantic childhood memories.

In 1975 Niels bought a farm called Thorshøjgaard on the north coast of Zealand, close to the holiday resort of Dronningmølle. Here he has about 63 hectares ranging from sand-hills to low-lying land, where he grows cereals, potatoes and root crops, and keeps black and white Landrace pigs, old Danish Landrace chickens and a flock of sheep of an old Scandinavian breed. He also has about fifty Danish Red dairy cows, representing one in five of the total Danish stock of this breed, which is threatened with extinction. The farm is run on the biodynamic principles laid down in the anthroposophical works of Rudolf Steiner. It can be hard to understand, let alone explain, how agriculture can be combined with a spiritual dimension, and if I were to try to do so in a few lines it would be far too banal and over-simplified. However, one thing is not hard to understand about biodynamics as practised by Niels Stokholm – you can taste the difference.

When I see the contact Niels has with his animals and the way he cares for them, I sometimes have a guilty conscience. After all, I bear some of the blame for them having to be slaughtered. But to be honest, the quality and the taste are in a league of their own. The pork has the fine structure of veal and a very complex and extremely unusual flavour, while the cows' milk is some of the most delicious I have ever tasted. A probable reason for this is the demonstrably greater diversity of plant and weed species in his meadows than anywhere else in the country.

Niels believes in the usefulness of every single plant, unlike many farmers who spray the land to get rid of their weeds. He also milks his cows only once a day, compared with the dairy industry's twice or three times. The cattle graze freely and only come home for milking and to drink water. In the winter, all the animals are fed on a nourishing, vitamin-rich diet of beet, corn and hay – all grown and harvested by Niels. What is more, the cows are not de-horned. In biodynamic farming, a cow's horns are thought to have an effect on the quality of their milk. There are blood vessels that run from the horns to the stomach, which in turn is connected to their metabolism, which directly affects a cow's milk production.

So Niels Stokholm's cows are not like most other cows. And Niels Stokholm is not like most people.

Photograph page 166

Susanne Grefberg
from
Gotland

I have never really enjoyed being fêted or receiving gifts. I don't know what the reason is, but even as a child I didn't feel comfortable at my birthday parties and on other occasions when I was the centre of attention. Yet I love it when other people are applauded: nice colleagues from restaurants who have done particularly well and are getting credit for it, for example, or seeing my little daughter's delight at being given a new box of paints. One of the things that has given me the greatest pleasure at Noma is seeing my employees being recognized for their hard work. For instance when Torsten Vildgaard, our sous-chef for six years, was honoured as Chef of the Year in Denmark and later won the prestigious Nordic Challenge. Or when Lau Richter, our restaurant manager and mastermind of the service department, was declared the best in the country. Or all the times when our brilliant sommelier, Pontus Elofsson, has received acclaim for his unique knowledge of wine, beer and drinks in general. Thinking about all the young women and men, whose success the restaurant has shared in makes it all seem worthwhile even at the most hectic moments.

The first time I had the pleasure of meeting Susanne, I needed something to cheer me up. It was in 2005, and I hadn't had a very good day at Noma. In fact the whole of the previous month had been unsatisfactory. I felt that the kitchen had been going around in circles for some time – we hadn't been constantly developing and we were starting to repeat ourselves. Sometimes it can be hard to break out of this kind of stagnation, but it's often the little things that can make a positive difference. For example, it happened one year when I picked the first wild garlic of the year myself – it gave me renewed energy and inspiration. And in 2005 it was Susanne, who became the muse of the kitchen. She contributed so much energy, drive and understanding that soon afterwards I decided to visit her at home on the Swedish island of Gotland, in the middle of the Baltic Sea between Sweden and the Baltic States.

Susanne is actually from Copenhagen, though she has been living on Gotland since 1976. A trained florist and English translator, she met her Swedish husband on holiday in Malta, and today she is more of a 'Scandinavian' – a nice mixture of the best of Denmark and Sweden. She has been a teacher and a student counsellor, and also worked for many years in the field of ship provisioning. Gradually she began to forage for food in the countryside and to grow her own berries, as the suppliers at the time did not come up to the standards she wanted to be able to deliver. Today she runs a smallholding with her son, concentrating mainly on root vegetables. In addition, she also collects a lot of plants, flowers and berries from the countryside. At Noma we mainly use her berries, her eggs from Swedish Blue ducks, her lamb, wild truffles, roses and oils.

Gotland has some 57,000 inhabitants, but that number doubles during the summer. The seasons arrive on the island at different times from the rest of Sweden, due to the fact that Gotland is situated to leeward of the Swedish mainland. This means that there is less rain and there are more hours of sunshine than anywhere else in Scandinavia. Gotland was created 400 million years ago by limestone deposits from dead sea creatures and corals in a tropical sea near the Equator. Since then, the underlying plate tectonics have pushed Gotland up into its present position. The high lime content of the soil explains the great wealth of wild plants and the varied landscape, with its 800 kilometres of coastline, its lakes and its large tracts of forest.

As Susanne showed me around the island I was struck by how fertile the landscape was. The long stretches of beach offer an abundance of marine plants and seaweed, and the fields and meadows are full of small berry-bearing bushes, trees and wild orchids. Susanne is familiar with every nook and cranny and knows where the very best things grow. It was here that I first tasted roasted mustard oil and small organic bantam and duck eggs. It was also on Gotland that I sampled little green shoots of whitebeam, blue raspberries and other berries in quantities and of a quality that are hard to find elsewhere. We tried rapeseed oil, which tasted like melted butter, as well as honey and barbecued wild leeks. It was a revelation to me. I remember sitting in my hotel room in the evening trying to sort out all the new impressions and flavours. Powerfully affected by everything I had experienced, I couldn't help smiling to myself as I felt this rare sense of satisfaction. My discovery was just crying out to be shared with someone, so I phoned home to the kitchen at Noma. But nobody answered. I lay down to sleep, and as I closed my eyes I thought: 'What a gift.'

Photograph page 181

K.S.
Møller
from
Zealand

In spring, summer and autumn, when nature is teeming with life and abundance, our chefs are out in the early mornings on the shores of Zealand or deep in a forest searching for sorrel, woodruff or wild berries. I love this morning ritual. To start the day by harvesting the fruits of nature while listening to birdsong or the roar of the waves is something special. And the outdoor experience is made even more special because we will be preparing and serving our new-found raw materials to our guests just a few hours later. Now, after almost seven years, we have drawn our own map of Zealand. The names of towns and streets have been replaced with the names of raw materials... there are bulrushes at Dronningmølle, wild garlic in Kongelunden, sea beet along the coast north of Dragsholm Castle, and so on.

Of course it hasn't always been like that. People often ask where we acquired our knowledge of wild plants. Obviously a lot can be learned by reading good specialist books and searching on the Internet. That helped us at the start – in addition, of course, to the knowledge I had gained from my job as sous-chef at the Kong Hans under head chef Thomas Rode Andersen. In fact, he was the first to open my eyes to all the wild raw materials that could be found in the Danish countryside. However, the major breakthrough came when I began working with K.S. Møller. I knew quite a lot about K.S. before Noma opened, but until then we hadn't had much contact. Luckily Mads Refslund, my friend and part of the Noma team for the first few months, was already in close contact with him through his job as head chef at the Paul in Copenhagen's Tivoli Gardens. So that's how K.S. Møller became associated with Noma right from the start in November 2003.

The child of Danish and Polish parents, he was born in 1944 in a small suburb of the city of Gdansk. As a five-year-old boy in Poland, he had what he describes as a revelation. While walking on his own, K.S. experienced a feeling of being bombarded by exciting sensual impressions as he looked over what he remembers as a completely unspoilt valley. It was as if something was calling him. The feeling lasted only a few minutes, but all the same it burned itself into the young boy's memory. He says that from that day on he knew that nature would have a special meaning in his life. In fact it was not until his thirties that his eyes were once again opened to the riches of the countryside. During a family trip to the beach, K.S. and an aunt made their way into a nearby wood while the rest of the family were bathing. It was an uneventful July day, and there had been a lot of rain that summer, K.S. recalls. The heavy rain had produced very favourable conditions for various midsummer mushrooms. K.S. and his aunt soon found some lovely little boletus with reddish pores.

However, later that day, when the rest of the family passed the spot where the beautiful boletus were growing, his father objected to them, saying that he knew from a book that the red underside of the boletus meant that the mushroom was poisonous. K.S.'s aunt was sure that, on the contrary, these particular mushrooms were edible. In the end, the mushrooms were left behind on his father's orders, but the discussion inspired K.S. to investigate who was actually right. After this he became more and more interested in mycology and in identifying the various species of woodland fungi. Incidentally, the aunt was right – the mushrooms were edible. The fungus in question was a *Boletus luridus*.

Today K.S. has two functions connected with Noma. For almost forty years he has been foraging in the wild, mainly for mushrooms, and in this time he has built up a unique knowledge of the appearance and growing conditions of the various species. Since 1995 he has also kept a diary in which he has noted the relationships between climate, weather conditions and the frequency with which each type of mushroom is found. As a result he now has a great instinct for what the weather will bring in the way of mushrooms and plants. Many Noma menus are only planned after consultation with K.S.

In addition, once or twice a year he takes cooks and apprentices from Noma with him on his mushroom walks. He considers it very important to share his knowledge of sustainability in respect of both fungi and herbs. For example, he gives guidance on the best time to pick the various species and how to do so without unnecessarily harming the vegetation. K.S. Møller takes good care of the countryside that the rest of us love to visit.

Photograph page 211

Tage
Rønne
from
Hareskovby

'It's only two weeks till birch sap time. That's what I think.' Such was the message that Tage Rønne left on my answering machine one raw March morning.

Waking up to this kind of greeting is one of the high spots of the year for me and the other chefs at Noma, because it's so much more than just a brief statement. The arrival of the birch sap is a guaranteed harbinger of spring. It means the end of root vegetables, onions and cabbage in every imaginable variation, the end of old apples and pears and extra-sweet beetroot. Thanks to Tage, spring had begun as far as I was concerned, because all kinds of other raw materials follow hard on the heels of the birch sap. A new season gradually begins to take shape, and wild garlic, ground elder, violets, Star of Bethlehem, seaweed, peas, shore plants, asparagus, lettuce, mushrooms, and so on will soon be out there waiting for us.

In a way, every year when Tage spreads more happiness and enthusiasm than anyone else on a cold March morning, it feels like a kind of gastronomic New Year's Eve. Today Tage is our inspiration and our driving force. He also supplies small green rowan shoots, which have the purest bitter almond taste you can imagine. He supplies bark from various woodland trees, though we mainly use wood shavings and bark from the birch. We use the wood and bark in almost everything – in infusions for oil, ice cream, bouillons and marinades. He also supplies us with spruce resin and shoots, and the range is extended year by year. It all began with the birch sap, which is now one of the cornerstones of Noma's cuisine, just like rye bread, horseradish and vinegar.

Birch sap is derived from the water sucked up from the ground by the tree's roots in early spring. The sap is tapped by boring a small hole through the bark into the heart of the tree. In this way several litres of sap can drip out over twenty-four hours. This usually continues over a period of no more than six weeks, so the sap is very seasonal. Once tapped, it keeps for only three or four days in the refrigerator, much like milk. It has a fresh taste and a slight natural sweetness due to the presence of fructose, glucose and xylitol.

In the restaurant we use the sap in a large number of dishes, and Tage himself says that it contains a natural flavour-enhancer. Maybe that's why it is so brilliant for cooking vegetables. They simply have more flavour, just as a dash of birch sap and vinegar can work wonders to freshen up a sauce. Our guests are served iced sap instead of iced water when the sap is in season. It's very refreshing when drunk ice-cold, and I have this slightly crazy idea that serving it with the food makes the dishes taste better and brings out their flavour more distinctly. We also brew our own beer from birch sap. It's a light pilsner type, in which we replace all the water with sap. We even have a homoeopath living in a nearby wood who makes birch wine for us. With the addition of a little apple and wine yeast, the natural sugar content of the sap gives a really fresh, tart 'wine' with a hint of rust that is slightly reminiscent of dry vermouth.

There is no doubting the fact that living and working outdoors really suits Tage. When he gives you his firm handshake you feel the roughness of his hands, and his hair resembles a wild bramble bush the colour of liver pâté. An open, out-going man, always positive and smiling, Tage was born in Ballerup near Copenhagen in 1956. Today he lives in Hareskovby, just three kilometres from his childhood home.

After leaving school, he trained as a woodman. Most of the work involved creating big plantations, but Tage wanted to work more closely with the trees and to do more for their well-being, so later he went back and trained as an arborist. Tage Rønne has really helped to shape Noma, just as the other producers and collaborators highlighted in this book have. The heart of our success lies in Tage's tenacity, in the great care he takes to continually deliver the highest quality ingredients, and in his connection to the profusion of materials that nature provides. Noma is intrinsically linked to Tage's birch sap, rowan berries and young shoots, amongst all the other brilliant raw materials that he gathers from the forest around him. In this way, my relationship with him is invaluable and my gratitude immeasurable.

Photograph page 234

EVERYONE
AT
NOMA

Photographs by
Ditte Isager

GLOSSARY

AGAR AGAR

A gelling agent derived from seaweed, which retains its gelling properties up to a temperature of 80°C (176°F).

ANGELICA

An edible plant that can be preserved (the stem), or eaten raw (the seeds and leaves).

AQUAVIT

A Scandinavian flavoured spirit, also known as akvavit.

BINTJE POTATO

A common variety of medium-sized potato that is grown extensively across Europe.

BIODYNAMIC

A method of farming which treats the farm as a separate, self-sustaining organism, with a natural, sustainable relationship between the soil, plants and animals, and the natural rhythms of the calendar.

BIRCH SYRUP

A syrup made from reducing the sap of birch trees.

BIRCH WATER

Sap from the birch tree.

BIRCH WINE

A wine made from the spring sap of the birch tree.

BLANCH

To cook food, often vegetables, briefly in boiling water. Usually followed by 'refreshing', or plunging straight into cold water to stop the food cooking.

BLAST FREEZER

An extremely cold freezer that can freeze food very quickly.

BLEAK

A small slender, silvery fish, its name deriving from the Old Norse word *bleikja*, meaning 'white colour'. It is similiar to the Vendace.

BLOOM (GELATINE)

To soften gelatine leaves by soaking them for a few minutes in cold water.

BORNHOLM

A Danish island in the Baltic Sea associated with a high quality type of flour produced from cereal crops that originate from the island.

BROWN BUTTER

A butter preparation with a nutty flavour, made by heating unsalted butter until it has browned to a hazelnut colour. Also known as *beurre noisette*.

BULRUSH

A grass-like marsh plant. The bulrush used at Noma is *Typha latifolia*, or 'common bulrush', not *Scirpus lacustris* (known as the 'true bulrush').

CLOUDBERRY

A berry, similar in appearance to the raspberry, which grows on small, shrub-like bushes across the Nordic region. They are first red, then turn deep orange, and finally pale yellow-orange when very ripe.

COUVERTURE CHOCOLATE

A type of chocolate with a very high percentage of cocoa butter, often used for coating other ingredients.

DEHYDRATOR

A kitchen appliance that removes the moisture content from food, thereby preserving it and decreasing its volume.

DOYENNÉ DU COMICE PEARS

A common dessert pear which is particularly large, juicy and sweet-flavoured.

DULSE

An edible seaweed, bright red in colour. Also known as Söl.

EINKORN

A wheat cereal, one of the first cultivated by humans for food, although not now grown extensively. It contains a high level of protein.

EMMER

A primitive wheat cereal, similar to einkorn.

EMULSIFY

To mix liquids of different densities together to form a thicker liquid.

FINGERLING POTATO

A variety of potato with a stubby, elongated shape. They grow to a similar size as new potatoes when fully mature.

GASTRO

Short for 'gastronorm', a type of deep metal tray used in professional kitchens for food storage and preparation, which are made in a range of standard sizes.

GELLAN GUM

A gelling agent that creates a very transparent gel.

GLACE

A strong-flavoured reduced brown stock, used to supply colour and body to sauces.

GLAZE

To coat food with a liquid to give it a glossy appearance.

GOOSEFOOT

A family of plants characterised by their ability to grow in salty conditions. Common edible varieties include Fat Hen, Good-King-Henry, and red goosefoot.

GRANITA

A frozen preparation, traditionally served as a dessert, made with water and a syrup base.

HAZELNUT FLOUR

A flour-like powder formed of ground hazelnuts.

HEN OF THE WOOD

A type (*Grifola frondosa*) of edible mushroom with dark brown caps, found in large clumps at the base of trees. Not to be confused with the chicken of the wood mushroom (*Laetiporus sulphurous*).

INSTANT FOOD THICKENER

A substance used to add texture to puréed foods and consistency to liquids.

ISOMALT

A sugar substitute which does not caramelize, as sugar does.

JACK BY THE HEDGE

A small, very common shrub, also known as garlic mustard, with a smell and taste of garlic.

JAPANESE TURNING VEGETABLE SLICER

A kitchen tool suitable for slicing vegetables into spiral shapes.

KAMUT

A type of wheat, related to durum wheat, with a high level of protein and a nutty taste.

LINGONBERRY

A bright red berry, similar to the cranberry, and also known as the cowberry. Appears on small evergreen shrubs and can be used as a preservative or as an ingredient in its own right.

LUMPFISH

A small fish, widespread in Arctic and North Atlantic waters, the roe of which can be eaten.

MALT FLOUR

A type of flour produced from ground malted cereals, such as barley, which imparts a natural sweetness.

MALTODEXTRINE

A starch-derived sugar, which can be used to give foods body and texture.

MANDOLIN

A kitchen tool with adjustable blades for thinly slicing vegetables and other food.

MEAD

An alcoholic drink made from honey.

MICROPLANE GRATER

A type of high-quality grater used in professional kitchens.

MUSTARD OIL

An oil obtained directly from mustard seeds, or by infusing vegetable oil with mustard seed extract.

MUTZU APPLE

A large variety of apple, closely related to the Golden Delicious, and with a similarly sweet taste.

MUIKKO

The Finnish word for the Vendace fish (see Bleak). It is generally salted and smoked.

MYCRYO

A powdered fat made from cocoa butter, which can be used for frying.

ÖLAND

A Swedish island associated with a high quality type of flour produced from cereal crops originating from the island.

PACO CONTAINERS

The receptacles used with a Pacojet.

PACOJET

A machine used to make sorbets with a very fine texture, as well as other creations such as frozen powders.

PARISIENNE CUTTER

A sharp-edged kitchen utensil used to cut out, or scoop, small balls of food.

QUARK

A type of soft, fresh, white coloured cheese, similar in consistency to cream cheese.

RAMSONS

Wild garlic, grows extensively in many parts of Europe and has a milder flavour than cultivated garlic.

RATTE POTATO

A small potato with a chestnut-like flavour and a particularly smooth texture.

RED CURRANT WINE

Wine produced from fermented red currants.

REFRACTOMETER

An instrument for measuring the refractive index, or sugar content, of a liquid, which is measured in degrees Brix.

ROSE CRESS

A small, herbaceous plant, also known as rose rock cress.

ROSE HIP VINEGAR

A vinegar prepared from combining a suitable vinegar (such as apple balsamic) with rose hips.

RUGOSA ROSES

A common variety of rose, with Latin name *Rosa rugosa*, which produces prominent hips and petals.

SEA BUCKTHORN

A wild shrub with bright orange edible berries, grows mainly on sand dunes and cliffs.

SEA KALE

A coastal plant, growing mainly on shingle beaches, with cabbage-like leaves.

SEA LETTUCE

A type of green seaweed that grows on rocks within intertidal areas of seashores across the world.

SEA PURSLANE

A shrub that grows on salt marshes, with salty-tasting leaves.

SILPAT

A non-stick silicone baking mat.

SIPHON

A utensil originally designed to whip cream and used in modern professional kitchens for the making of foams.

SKYR

A mildly sour-tasting milk product, similar to strained yoghurt, although technically it is a very soft cheese. Skyr is popular in Iceland and Denmark.

SLAKE

To mix powdered ingredients such as flour to a smooth paste with a little cold liquid, before adding to a hot mixture.

SÖL

Another name for dulse.

SPECK

Fat from the back of a pig, available untreated, raw or smoked.

SPELT

A wheat cereal with a nutty taste. Spelt flour is able to absorb greater amounts of water than standard flour.

SPRUCE SHOOTS

Shoots of the spruce tree.

STONECROP

A berry-producing family of plants characterised by their ability to grow on rocks and stony ground. Edible varieties include white stonecrop, reflexed stonecrop and orpine.

SWEET CICELY

A small plant with fine, green, lacy leaves with an aniseed taste. Not to be confused with hemlock, which is a relative, has similar leaves, and can be poisonous.

SUPERBAG

A very fine mesh bag through which liquids can be strained and clarified.

THERMOMIX

A food processor that can blend food at different temperatures.

THUJA CONES

Cones of the thuja tree, also known as the arborvitae, which emerge as small buds and grow to 1–2 cm-long brown cones.

TOPAZ APPLE

A variety of apple, notable for its sharp taste.

TRIMOLINE

A type of sugar-based sweetener, used by many chefs in baking and in sorbets.

TRUFFLE SLICER

A utensil with a fine, very sharp, adjustable blade, used to slice truffles to various thicknesses.

VÄSTERBOTTEN CHEESE

A type of hard cheese produced in Sweden with a salty, bitter taste.

VINEGAR POWDER

A powdered form of vinegar, used to add the flavour of vinegar without adding further liquid to a dish.

WATER BATH

In its simplest form, a vessel of hot water in which foods can be cooked gently, as in a bain marie. Many professional kitchens use a Roner, which can maintain temperatures very accurately for long periods.

WOODRUFF

A plant that grows in large clumps on woodland floors, the leaves taste similar to vanilla.

XANTHAN GUM

A product derived from fermented starch, used as a thickening agent and to maintain solids in suspension within a liquid.

ZITTAUER ONION

A common variety of onion that is cultivated in the Nordic regions.

INDEX

Page numbers in brackets refer to photographs

Notes on the recipes

All recipes serve four people.

A number of the recipes require advanced techniques, specialist equipment and professional experience to achieve good results.

Cooking times are for guidance only. If using a fan oven, follow the manufacturer's instructions concerning the oven temperatures.

Eggs are medium size, unless specified. Some recipes include lightly cooked eggs, meat and fish. These should be avoided by the elderly, infants, pregnant women, convalescents and anyone with an impaired immune system.

Exercise a very high level of caution when following recipes involving any potentially hazardous activity, including the use of high temperatures, open flames and when deep frying. In particular, when deep frying add food carefully to avoid splashing, wear long sleeves and never leave the pan unattended. Liquid nitrogen is a dangerous substance and should not be handled without training in how to use it safely.

Exercise caution when foraging for ingredients. Any foraged ingredients should only be eaten if an expert has deemed them safe to eat.

All spoon measurements are level. 1 teaspoon = 5 ml. 1 tablespoon = 15ml. Australian standard tablespoons are 20 ml; Australian readers are advised to use 3 teaspoons in place of 1 tablespoon.

Phaidon Press Limited
Regent's Wharf
All Saints Street
London N1 9PA

Phaidon Press Inc.
180 Varick Street
New York, NY 10014

www.phaidon.com

First published 2010
© 2010 Phaidon Press Limited

ISBN 978 0 7148 5903 3

A CIP catalogue record for this book is
available from the British Library

Photographs by Ditte Isager
Photographs styled by Christine Rudolph
Designed by Studio Frith
Map illustration by Hannah Warren

Printed in China